A-LEVEL
STUDENT GUIDE

AQA

Physical Education

Factors affecting optimal performance in physical activity and sport

Symond Burrows
Michaela Byrne
Sue Young

Hodder Education, an Hachette UK company, Blenheim Court, George Street, Banbury, Oxfordshire OX16 5BH

Orders

Bookpoint Ltd, 130 Park Drive, Milton Park, Abingdon, Oxfordshire OX14 4SB

tel: 01235 827827

fax: 01235 400401

e-mail: education@bookpoint.co.uk

Lines are open 9.00 a.m.–5.00 p.m., Monday to Saturday, with a 24-hour message answering service. You can also order through the Hodder Education website: www.hoddereducation.co.uk

ISBN 978-1-5104-5549-8

First printed 2019

Impression number 5 4 3 2 1

Year 2023 2022 2021 2020 2019

This Student Guide has been written specifically to support students preparing for the AQA A-level examinations. The content has been neither approved nor endorsed by AQA and remains the sole responsibility of the author.

Typeset by Integra Software Services Pvt. Ltd., Pondicherry, India

Printed in Dubai

Cover photograph: biker 3

Hachette UK's policy is to use papers that are natural, renewable and recyclable products and made from wood grown in well-managed forests and other controlled sources. The logging and manufacturing processes are expected to conform to the environmental regulations of the country of origin.

Contents

Content Guidance

Questions and Answers

■ Getting the most from this book

Exam tips
Advice on key points in the text to help you learn and recall content, avoid pitfalls, and polish your exam technique in order to boost your grade.

Knowledge check
Rapid-fire questions throughout the Content Guidance section to check your understanding.

Knowledge check answers
1 Turn to the back of the book for the Knowledge check answers.

Summaries
■ Each core topic is rounded off by a bullet-list summary for quick-check reference of what you need to know.

Exam-style questions

Commentary on the questions
Tips on what you need to do to gain full marks.

Sample student answers
Practise the questions, then look at the student answers that follow.

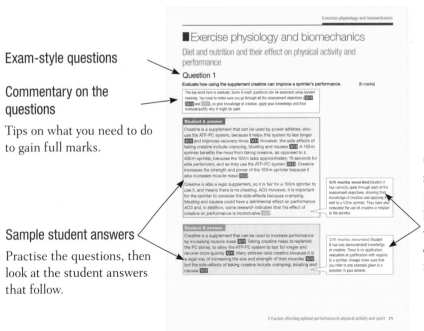

Commentary on sample student answers
Read the comments showing how many marks each answer would be awarded in the exam and exactly where marks are gained or lost.

■ About this book

This Student Guide covers the topics required for AQA A-level specification 7582 Paper 2: Factors affecting optimal performance in physical activity and sport. Remember that this is a guide, not a textbook. It provides a succinct summary of what you need to know and understand for your exam, but is intended to complement, not replace, your textbook and class notes.

■ How to use the book

The first section, Content Guidance, follows the headings set out in the AQA specification. It is divided into three main topic areas:

- Exercise physiology and biomechanics
- Sport psychology
- Sport and society and the role of technology in physical activity and sport

To help aid your revision, each topic area in the Content Guidance includes exam tips, knowledge check questions and definitions of some key terms. Use the knowledge checks as you progress through the guide to test your understanding, and take on board the exam tips to avoid falling into the traps that most commonly result in students losing marks. At the end of each topic area there is a summary of the content covered. If you are unable to offer a detailed explanation of any part of this, you should work through this section again to clear up any misunderstanding.

The second section, Questions & Answers, begins by setting out the format of the exam papers, giving you advice and important tips on how to maximise your marks on the different elements of the paper. It also explains the levels system used for extended questions.

This is followed by a series of sample questions. These are all accompanied by example student answers, some illustrating best practice with others showing how *not* to answer the questions. You should attempt all of these questions yourself and compare your answers with the examples, while reading the detailed comments to help improve your understanding of what is required to achieve top marks.

Content Guidance

■ Exercise physiology and biomechanics

Diet and nutrition and their effect on physical activity and performance

The exercise-related function of food classes

Carbohydrate

Carbohydrates are the principal source of energy used by the body. Glycogen and glucose provide the fuel for both aerobic and anaerobic energy production. Glucose is stored in the muscles and liver as glycogen, but these stores are limited, so regular refuelling is necessary.

Fibre

Fibre is important during exercise because it can slow down the time it takes the body to break down food, which results in a slower, more sustained release of energy. Dietary fibre causes bulk in the small intestine, helping to prevent constipation and aiding digestion.

Fat

Fats can only be broken down for aerobic energy production, but have twice the energy yield of carbohydrates. Trans fats allow food to have a longer shelf life, but can lead to high levels of blood cholesterol, heart disease and diabetes. Too much saturated fat leads to weight gain, which can affect stamina, limit flexibility and lead to health problems, such as coronary heart disease, diabetes and high blood pressure. Not all fats are bad. Replacing saturated and trans fats with unsaturated fats is important because fat is a major source of energy in the body. Fats are also a carrier for the fat-soluble vitamins A, D, E and K.

Cholesterol is a type of fat found in the blood. Too much saturated fat leads to high cholesterol levels. Cholesterol is made predominantly in the liver and is carried in the blood as **LDL** (low-density lipoprotein) and **HDL** (high-density lipoprotein).

LDL (bad cholesterol) is transported in the blood to the tissues. Too much can lead to fatty deposits developing in the arteries, which can have a negative effect on blood flow.

HDL (good cholesterol), when in excess, is transported in the blood back to the liver, where it is broken down.

Protein

Amino acids from proteins are a minor source of energy and are more important for muscle growth and repair and to make enzymes, hormones and haemoglobin.

Vitamins

For your exam you need to know the exercise-related functions of vitamins C and D, and the B complex, which includes several important vitamins (Table 1).

Table 1 The exercise-related functions of vitamins C and D, and the B complex

Vitamin	Source	Exercise-related function
C (ascorbic acid)	Green vegetables and fruit	Protects cells and keeps them healthy Helps in the maintenance of bones, teeth, gums and connective tissue, for example ligaments Required for the breakdown of carnitine, a molecule essential for the transport of fatty acids into the mitochondria; it is the mitochondria that convert food sources (such as fats) into energy in the body
D	Made by the body from sunlight and from oily fish/dairy produce	Has a role in the absorption of calcium, which keeps bones and teeth healthy Helps with phosphocreatine recovery in the mitochondria
Vitamin B complex (selected examples)		
B1 (thiamin)	Yeast, egg, liver, wholegrain bread, nuts, red meat	Works with other B group vitamins to help break down and release energy from food Keeps the nervous system healthy
B2 (riboflavin)	Dairy, liver, vegetables, eggs, cereals, fruit	Works with other B group vitamins to help break down and release energy from food Keeps the skin, eyes and nervous system healthy
B6	Meat, fish, eggs, vegetables, cereals	Helps form haemoglobin Helps the body to use and store energy from protein and carbohydrate in food
B12 (folate)	Red meat, fish, dairy	Helps in the formation of red blood cells, and keeps the nervous system healthy Releases energy from food

Minerals

For your exam, you need to know the exercise-related functions of the following minerals:

- Calcium — for strong bones and teeth/for efficient nerve and muscle function.
- Sodium — regulates fluid levels in the body. Too much can lead to an increase in blood pressure, which increases risk of a stroke/heart attack.
- Iron — helps the formation of haemoglobin in red blood cells, which transport oxygen. Lack of iron leads to anaemia.

Water

Water transports nutrients, hormones and waste products around the body, and regulates body temperature. Blood plasma is 90% water and carries glucose to the respiring muscles. During exercise water is lost in the cooling down process. A lack of water before, during or after exercise can cause dehydration; this can result in a decrease in plasma volume and stroke volume, and an increase in temperature and heart rate. As a result, performance will deteriorate.

Positive and negative effects of dietary supplements/manipulation on the performer

Creatine

This is a supplement used to increase the amount of phosphocreatine stored in the muscles. Phosphocreatine is used to fuel the ATP-PC system, which provides energy.

Exam tip

Make sure that you can evaluate the use of each of the food groups during both aerobic and anaerobic exercise.

Knowledge check 1

How might the diet of a sedentary individual differ from that of an endurance athlete and a power athlete?

Increasing the amount of creatine in the muscles allows this energy system to last longer. It can also help improve muscle mass and recovery times. Creatine is most suitable for athletes in explosive events such as sprinting. Negative side effects are bloating, muscle cramps, diarrhoea, water retention and vomiting. There is also mixed evidence on the benefits of creatine.

Sodium bicarbonate

Sodium bicarbonate is an antacid. It can increase the buffering capacity of the blood, and so can neutralise the negative effects of the lactic acid and hydrogen ions that are produced in the muscles during high-intensity activity, thus delaying fatigue. Negative side-effects include vomiting, pain, cramping, diarrhoea and bloating.

Caffeine

Caffeine is a naturally occurring stimulant, which can increase mental alertness and reduce fatigue. It is also thought to improve the mobilisation of fatty acids in the body, thereby sparing muscle glycogen stores. It is used by endurance performers who predominantly rely on the aerobic system, because fats are the preferred fuel for low-intensity, long-endurance exercise. However, caffeine can lead to a loss of fine control, dehydration, insomnia, muscle cramps, vomiting and diarrhoea.

Glycogen loading

Glycogen loading is a form of dietary manipulation to increase the amount of glycogen stored over and above that which can normally be stored (**supercompensation**).

- **Method one** — 6 days before competition, the performer eats a diet high in protein for 3 days and exercises at relatively high intensity to burn off any existing carbohydrate stores. This is followed by 3 days of a diet high in carbohydrates and some light training. The theory is that by totally depleting glycogen stores they can then be increased by up to twice the original amount (supercompensation), and can prevent the performer from 'hitting the wall'.
- **Method two** — the day before competition, 3 minutes of high-intensity exercise opens a 'carbo window'. Replenishing glycogen stores during the first 20-minute window after exercise can enhance performance the next day. In the 20 minutes immediately after exercise, the body is most able to restore lost glycogen. The 'carbo window' closes after 2 hours.
- **Method three** — in this non-depletion protocol, training intensity is reduced the week before competition. Then 3 days before competition a high-carbohydrate diet is followed by low-intensity exercise.

Disadvantages during the carbo-loading phase are that performers may experience water retention, bloating, heavy legs and weight increase, and during the depletion phase irritability and a lack of energy.

> **Exam tip**
>
> Remember that creatine is important in extending the use of the ATP-PC system.

> **Exam tip**
>
> A common mistake is to say that caffeine *increases* reaction time — it does not. It *improves* reaction time.

> **Glycogen loading** is the manipulation of carbohydrate intake in the week before a competition to maximise stores of glycogen.
>
> **Supercompensation** involves maximising muscle glycogen stores before endurance events.

Summary

After studying this topic you should be able to:
- understand the exercise-related functions of carbohydrate, fibre, fat (saturated fat, trans fat and cholesterol), proteins, vitamins (C, D, B-complex), minerals (sodium, iron, calcium) and water
- identify the positive and negative effects of creatine, sodium bicarbonate, caffeine and glycogen loading on the performer

Preparation and training methods in relation to maintaining physical activity and performance

Key terms relating to laboratory conditions and field tests
- Quantitative data are measured and recorded numerically.
- Qualitative data are descriptive and record the way people think or feel.
- Objective data are based upon facts and are measurable.
- Subjective data are based on opinion.
- Validity refers to the degree to which a test actually measures what it sets out to.
- Reliability refers to the degree to which a test can be repeated accurately.

Physiological effects and benefits of a warm-up and cool-down
A warm-up helps prepare the body for exercise and consists of a pulse raiser, stretching and game-related activities. The benefits of a warm-up are as follows:
- It reduces the possibility of injury.
- It increases the elasticity of the muscle.
- Synovial fluid is released.
- Muscle temperature is increased.
- Increased blood flow to muscle tissues leads to better oxygen delivery.
- Increased speed of nerve conduction improves reaction time.
- It allows for the rehearsal of movement patterns used in the activity.
- It allows mental rehearsal.

The physiological benefits of a cool-down are as follows:
- It keeps the skeletal muscle pump working.
- This maintains venous return and prevents blood pooling in the veins.
- It removes lactic acid.
- It limits the effect of **DOMS**.

Stretching for different types of physical activity
Static stretching is when the muscle is held in a stationary position for 30 seconds or more. It can be *passive*, when a stretch occurs with the help of an external force, such as a partner, gravity or a wall, or *active*, where opposing muscles are used to push the joint beyond its point of resistance, lengthening the muscles and surrounding connective tissue.

Ballistic stretching involves performing a stretch with swinging or bouncing movements to push a body part even further, and is suitable for activities in which a large force of contraction is needed. However, it can be dangerous if not done correctly, and there is a risk of injury if the performer is not very flexible.

Principles of training

SPORR principles
- **S**pecificity — choosing the relevant training (same energy system, muscle fibre type, skills and movements).

Exam tip

Quantity requires a number and quality requires an opinion.

Exam tip

The multi-stage fitness test is objective because it is measurable, i.e. it measures the level achieved. It is valid for games players but is less valid for a swimmer or cyclist because the muscles are used in a different way, and swimming and cycling are not weight bearing.

Knowledge check 2

Why would the Cooper 12-minute run be a less valid test for a cyclist?

DOMS stands for delayed onset of muscle soreness, where pain and stiffness are usually felt 24–48 hours after exercise.

Exam tip

Make sure you can discuss the suitability of each type of stretching for different performers.

- **P**rogressive **O**verload — gradually training harder throughout a training programme as fitness improves (heavier weights, longer training sessions, greater distances).
- **R**eversibility — often referred to as detraining. Stop training and the level of fitness deteriorates.
- **R**ecovery — rest days are needed to allow the body to recover from training.

FITT principles

- **F**requency — you need to train often to improve.
- **I**ntensity — to improve you must train harder.
- **T**ime spent training — this needs to gradually increase.
- **T**ype of training — using different forms of exercise maintains motivation, but the type chosen needs to be relevant to your chosen activity.

Knowledge check 3

How can frequency be applied to a training programme?

Application of the principles of periodisation

Periodisation involves dividing the training year into blocks or sections in which specific training occurs. There are three main cycles: macro, meso and micro.

- A **macrocycle** is a long-term performance goal and can be divided into:
  - preparation period — similar to pre-season training, where fitness is developed
  - competition period — the performance period in which skills and techniques are refined and fitness is maintained.
  - transition period — the end of the season, when rest and recovery take place
- A **mesocycle** is usually a 4–12 week period of training with a particular focus, such as power. A 100 m sprinter, for example, will focus on power, reaction time and speed.
- A **microcycle** involves a training programme of 1 week or a few days that is repeated throughout the length of the mesocycle.

Tapering and peaking

Tapering involves reducing the volume and/or intensity of training prior to competition. Planning and organising training in this way prepares the athlete both physically and mentally for a major competition, and allows peaking to occur.

Training methods to improve physical fitness and health

For your exam you need to be able to explain each type of training, identify how it improves fitness and evaluate its effectiveness:

- **HIIT/Interval training** is used to improve anaerobic power. Periods (intervals) of high-intensity work are followed by active recovery periods.
- **Continuous training** develops aerobic endurance and involves low-intensity exercise for long periods of time, for example jogging.
- **Fartlek** also develops aerobic endurance and is a type of continuous training in which the intensity of the activity is varied. This overloads both the aerobic and anaerobic energy systems.
- **Proprioceptive neuromuscular facilitation** (**PNF**) is an advanced stretching technique. It is a form of passive stretching, in which the stretch position is held by something other than the agonist muscles, for example, a partner or a wall.

Knowledge check 4

Why is fartlek training a relevant method of training for a games player?

- **Weight training** develops muscular strength. It involves doing a series of resistance exercises through the use of free weights or fixed weight machines, which tend to be described in terms of sets and repetitions.
- **Circuit training** develops muscular endurance using a series of exercises at a set of 'stations'.

Summary

After studying this topic you should be able to:
- understand the terms quantitative, qualitative, objective, subjective, validity and reliability in relation to laboratory conditions and field tests
- explain the physiological benefits of a warm-up and cool-down
- explain the principles of training (SPORR and FITT)
- understand and be able to apply the principles of periodisation
- explain how HITT/interval, continuous, fartlek, circuit, weight and PNF training can improve physical fitness

Injury prevention and the rehabilitation of injury

Exam tip

Remember that a strain occurs in the muscle, whereas a sprain occurs in ligaments.

Types of injury

Acute injury

An acute injury is a sudden injury caused by a specific impact or traumatic event, where a sharp pain is felt immediately (Table 2).

Table 2 Acute injuries

Fracture	Dislocation	Strain	Sprain
A break or a crack in a bone is a fracture	Dislocations occur at joints and are very painful	Strains refer to 'pulled' or 'torn' muscles	Sprains occur to ligaments (strong bands of tissue around joints that join bone to bone) when they are stretched too far and tear
A simple or closed fracture is a clean break to a bone that does not penetrate through the skin or damage any surrounding tissue	They happen when the ends of bones are forced out of position	A strain occurs when muscle fibres are stretched too far and tear	
A compound or open fracture is when the soft tissue or skin has been damaged; this is more serious because there is a higher risk of infection			

Chronic injury

Chronic injuries are often referred to as overuse injuries, and occur after playing sport or exercise for a long time (Table 3).

Achilles tendonitis is inflammation of the tendon joining the calf muscle to the heel.

Table 3 Chronic injuries

Achilles tendonitis	Stress fracture	'Tennis elbow'
Tendonitis causes pain and inflammation of the tendon	Stress fractures are most common in the weight-bearing bones of the legs, often when there is a rapid increase in the amount or intensity of exercise or activity	Tennis elbow occurs in the muscles attached to the elbow that are used to straighten the wrist
The achilles tendon is at the back of the ankle and is the largest tendon in the body. It connects the gastrocnemius to the heel bone and is used for walking, running and jumping, so when we do a lot of regular activity it can be prone to tendonitis	Muscles become fatigued, so they are no longer able to absorb the added shock of exercise	The muscles and tendons become inflamed and tiny tears occur on the outside of the elbow
	The fatigued muscle eventually transfers the stress overload to the bone, and the result is a tiny crack called a stress fracture	The area becomes very sore and tender
	The area becomes tender and swollen	Any activity that places repeated stress on the elbow, through overuse of the muscles and tendons of the forearm, can cause tennis elbow

Methods used in injury prevention, rehabilitation and recovery

Injury prevention

- Screening can help identify those at risk of complications from exercise, prepare performers for their sport, enhance performance and reduce injury. It can be used to detect a problem early before any symptoms occur. Screening can also save lives, for example **CRY**. However, some screening tests are not 100% accurate and may miss a problem. It can also increase anxiety when an athlete finds out they have a health problem or are more susceptible to injury.
- Wearing the correct protective equipment can help reduce injuries in sport (e.g. ankle shin pads in football).
- Warm-up (see preparation and training, p. 9).
- Flexibility training (see section on stretching, p. 9).
- Taping a weak joint helps with support and stability, whereas bracing is more substantial than taping, often involving hinged supports, and is used to give extra stability to muscles and joints that are weak or have been previously injured.

CRY (Cardiac Risk in the Young) is an echocardiogram screening programme for all young people between the ages of 14 and 35.

Injury rehabilitation

- Proprioceptive training involves hopping, jumping and balancing exercises to restore lost proprioception and teach the body to control the position of an injured joint subconsciously (e.g. balance boards for a sprained ankle).
- Strength training uses resistance of some kind to prepare the body for exercise. This resistance can be from weight machines, free weights, body weight or thera bands.
- Hydrotherapy is the use of warm water (35–37°C) to treat injuries. It improves blood circulation, relieves pain and relaxes muscles. The buoyancy of the water helps to support body weight, which reduces the load on joints.

Exam tip

Proprioceptive training and strength training are easily accessible.

Recovery from exercise

- Compression garments are generally used by athletes to help blood lactate removal and reduce both inflammation and the symptoms associated with DOMS (delayed onset muscle soreness).
- Sports massage can prevent or relieve **soft tissue** injuries. It increases blood flow to soft tissue, so that more oxygen and nutrients can pass through to help repair any damage, removes lactic acid, stretches soft tissue to relieve tension and pressure, and breaks down scar tissue, which if not removed can lead to mobility problems in soft tissue.
- Foam rollers are similar to self-massage.
- Cold therapy involves cooling the surface of the skin using ice. This gives pain relief and causes vasoconstriction of the blood vessels, which decreases blood flow and reduces any bleeding or swelling. A decrease in swelling enables the muscle to have more movement. Ice can also reduce muscle spasms by decreasing motor activity because the speed of the nerve impulse slows down in cold conditions.
- Ice baths are used by sports performers for 5–10 minutes after a gruelling training session or match. The cold water causes the blood vessels to tighten (vasoconstriction) and therefore reduces blood flow to the area. On leaving the bath the legs fill up with new blood (vasodilation), which invigorates the muscles with oxygen.

Soft tissue includes tendons, ligaments, muscles, nerves and blood vessels.

Physiological reasons for methods used in injury rehabilitation

- Hyperbaric chambers reduce the recovery time for an injury. The chamber is pressurised (in some chambers a mask is worn) and there is 100% pure oxygen. The pressure increases the amount of oxygen that can be breathed in and diffused to the injured area. The excess oxygen dissolves into the blood plasma, where it reduces swelling, stimulates white blood cell activity and increases blood supply at the injury site.

- Cryotherapy uses cold temperatures to treat injuries. Whole-body cryotherapy (WBC) involves the use of a cryogenic chambers to reduce pain and inflammation. The chamber is cooled by liquid nitrogen to a temperature below −100°C and the patient remains in the chamber, protected with socks, gloves and a swimming costume, for up to 3 minutes. The freezing gas surrounds the body so that the blood from the arms and legs flows towards the core in an attempt to keep the body warm and protect vital organs from the extreme cold. On leaving the chamber, the blood returns to the arms and legs full of oxygen, which helps to heal injured cells.

For common sporting injuries such as muscle strains, treatment is **PRICE**, where the ice has an analgesic effect and can limit pain and swelling by decreasing blood flow to the injured area.

PRICE is an acronym for Protection, Rest, Ice, Compression and Elevation.

Importance of sleep and nutrition for improved recovery

Deep sleep is important for muscle recovery. The deepest part of sleep is the third stage of **non-REM sleep**. Here, brain waves are at their slowest and blood flow is directed away from the brain towards the muscles to restore energy. If sleep is too short, then the time for repair is also cut short. Most elite athletes have a minimum of 8–9 hours sleep each night, but your body will tell you if you need more.

Nutrition is also crucial for recovery after exercise. During exercise muscle glycogen stores decrease, so they need to be replenished when exercise is finished. Research shows that replenishing glycogen stores during the first 20-minute window after exercise can then enhance performance the next day. In the 20 minutes immediately after exercise, the body is most able to restore lost glycogen.

Non-REM sleep consists of three stages of sleep that get progressively deeper. (REM stands for rapid eye movement.)

Knowledge check 5

How would you treat a muscle strain?

Knowledge check 6

Why is sleep important for improved recovery?

Summary

After studying this topic you should be able to:

- identify acute and chronic injuries
- understand how screening, protective equipment, warm-up, flexibility training, taping and bracing are used in injury prevention
- describe how proprioceptive training, strength training and hydrotherapy can help rehabilitation
- give the physiological reasons why hyperbaric chambers and cryotherapy are used in injury rehabilitation
- explain how compression garments, massage/foam rollers, cold therapy, ice baths and cryotherapy can aid recovery
- explain the importance of sleep and nutrition for improved recovery

Biomechanical principles

Newton's three laws of linear motion applied to sporting movements

- **Newton's first law of inertia**: 'Every body continues in its state of rest or motion in a straight line, unless compelled to change that state by external forces exerted upon it.' In a penalty, the ball (body) will remain on the spot (state of rest) unless it is kicked by the player (an external force is exerted upon it).
- **Newton's second law of acceleration**: 'The rate of momentum of a body (or the acceleration for a body of constant mass) is proportional to the force causing it and the change that takes place in the direction in which the force acts.'

  force = mass × acceleration ($F = ma$)

  When the player kicks (force) the ball during the game, the acceleration of the ball (rate of change of momentum) is proportional to the size of the force. So, the harder the ball is kicked, the further and faster it will go.
- **Newton's third law of action/reaction**: 'To every action force there is an equal and opposite reaction force.' When a footballer jumps up (action) to win a header, a force is exerted on the ground in order to gain height. At the same time the ground exerts an upward force (equal and opposite reaction) upon the player.

Centre of mass

The human body is an irregular shape, so the **centre of mass** cannot be identified easily. In addition, the body is constantly changing position, so the centre of mass will change as a result. In general, the centre of mass for someone adopting a standing position is in the region between the hips, and is slightly higher in females than in males.

Factors affecting stability

The following factors will affect stability:

- The height of the centre of mass — lowering the centre of mass will increase stability.
- Position of the line of gravity — this should be central over the base of support to increase stability.
- Area of the support base — the more contact points there are, the larger the base of support becomes, increasing stability. For example, a headstand has more contact points than a handstand, so is a more balanced position.
- Mass of the performer — often, the greater the mass, the more stability there is because of increased inertia.

Summary

After studying this topic you should be able to:
- identify Newton's first law (inertia), second law (acceleration) and third law (action/reaction), and apply these laws to sporting examples
- explain the centre of mass
- identify the factors that affect stability as height of centre of mass, area of base of support, position of line of gravity and body mass

Newton's first law of inertia states that a force is required to change the state of motion.

Newton's second law of acceleration states that the magnitude (size) and direction of the force determines the magnitude and direction of the acceleration.

Newton's third law of action/reaction states that for every action force there is an equal and opposite reaction force.

Exam tip

Make sure you can give a sporting example for each law of motion.

Centre of mass is the point of balance of a body.

Exam tip

Make sure that you can identify which law is which, because an exam question may ask for a specific law, for example: 'Using Newton's first law of motion…'.

Knowledge check 7

How can a rugby player increase their stability as they are about to tackle an opponent?

Levers

Three classes of lever and examples of their use in the body during physical activity and sport

There are three classes of lever: first, second and third. The classification of each depends on the positions of the fulcrum, resistance and effort in relation to each other.

First-class levers

Here, the fulcrum lies between the effort and the resistance (Figure 1). There are two examples of this type of lever in the body: the movement of the head and neck during flexion and extension, and extension of the elbow.

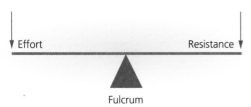

Figure 1 First-class lever

Second-class levers

In second-class levers, the resistance lies between the fulcrum and the effort (Figure 2). There is only one example of this type of lever in the body — plantar flexion of the ankle.

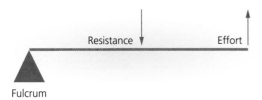

Figure 2 Second-class lever

Third-class levers

Third-class levers can be found in all the other joints of the body. The effort lies between the fulcrum and the resistance (Figure 3).

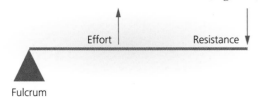

Figure 3 Third-class lever

Exam tip

Remember the mnemonic 'FRE 123', where 123 is the type of lever and FRE refers to the component that is in the middle. So, for example F for fulcrum is the first letter, so when the fulcrum is in the middle it is a first-class lever.

Mechanical advantages and disadvantages of each class of lever

Table 4 The mechanical advantages and disadvantages of each class of lever

Class of lever	Mechanical advantages	Mechanical disadvantages
Second	Can generate much larger forces Can lift the whole body weight	Slow, with a limited range of movement
First and third	Large range of movement Any resistance can be moved quickly	Cannot apply much force to move an object

Summary

After studying this topic you should be able to:
- identify the three classes of lever and give examples of their use in the body during physical activity and sport
- explain the mechanical advantages and disadvantages of each class of lever

Linear motion

Linear motion is motion in a straight or curved line, with all body parts moving the same distance, at the same speed and in the same direction.

The forces acting on a performer during linear motion

There are two types of **force**:
- An internal force is applied when our skeletal muscles contract.
- An external force comes from outside the body, for example **friction**, air resistance and weight.

Friction

Static friction occurs before an object starts to slide, whereas sliding friction acts between two surfaces that are moving relative to one another. Friction can be affected by the following factors:
- The surface characteristics of the two bodies in contact, for example a 100 m sprinter wears running spikes to increase friction with the track.
- The temperature of the two surfaces in contact. In curling, for example, the ice is often swept in front of the curling stone. The sweeping action slightly raises the surface temperature of the ice, which reduces the friction between the stone and ice, allowing the stone to travel further.
- The mass of the object that is sliding. A larger mass results in greater friction.

Air resistance

Air resistance opposes the motion of a body travelling through the air and depends upon:
- the velocity of the moving body
- the cross-sectional area of the moving body
- the shape and surface characteristics of the moving body

Weight

Weight is a gravitational force that the Earth exerts on a body, pulling it towards the centre of the Earth or effectively downwards.

Knowledge check 8

Plantar flexion of the ankle is important during the take-off in the high jump. Identify the class of lever that is used during this joint action and explain its mechanical advantage.

A **force** changes a body's state of motion.

Friction occurs when two or more bodies are in contact with one another.

Exam tip

A cyclist reduces their cross-sectional area by leaning forward over the handlebars.

Exam tip

Friction and air resistance are horizontal forces, whereas weight is a vertical force.

How forces act upon the performer during linear motion

Forces are vectors, so how they act upon a performer can be shown using an arrow on a free-body diagram. The position, direction and length of the arrow are important, and need to be drawn accurately. The length of the arrow drawn reflects the magnitude or size of the force. The longer the arrow, the bigger the size of the force (Figure 4).

Exam tip

To show how a weight force acts on a performer, an arrow can be drawn vertically downwards from the centre of mass.

Figure 4 From left to right: F (force) = AR (air resistance), so the net force is zero and there is a constant velocity; F > AR shows acceleration; F < AR shows deceleration

The effects of internal and external forces can be represented as a vector diagram. In the high jump, the performer uses a large internal muscular force from the leg muscles to create a big action force in order to achieve as much vertical displacement (height) as possible (Figure 5). The relationship between the amount of vertical force and horizontal force provided by the muscles will lean towards the vertical component (V). A long jumper, however, is trying to achieve as much horizontal distance as possible (Figure 6). This means there will be a greater contribution to the overall force from the horizontal component (H).

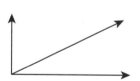

Figure 5 A vector diagram showing the resultant forces for the high jump

Figure 6 A vector diagram showing the resultant forces for the long jump

Knowledge check 9

Identify and explain two external forces acting on a sprinter.

Definitions, equations and units of vectors and scalars

Measurements used in linear motion can be divided into **scalar** and **vector quantities** (Table 5).

A **scalar quantity** is represented when measurements are described only in terms of size or magnitude, for example mass, distance and speed.

A **vector quantity** is represented when measurements are described in terms of magnitude (size) *and* direction, for example weight, acceleration, displacement, velocity and momentum.

Table 5 Definitions, equations and units of measurements for scalars and vectors

Measurements of linear motion	Definition	Unit of measurement	How to calculate (if relevant)
Mass	Mass is the quantity of matter the body possesses	Kg	–
Distance	Distance is the path a body takes as it moves from the starting to the finishing position.	Metres (m)	–
Speed	Speed is a measurement of the body's movement per unit of time, with no reference to direction	Metres per second (m/s)	$\text{speed} = \dfrac{\text{distance covered (m)}}{\text{time taken (s)}}$
Weight	Weight is the gravitational force exerted on an object	Newtons (N)	weight (N) = mass (kg) × gravitational field strength (N/kg)
Displacement	Displacement is the shortest route in a straight line between the starting and finishing position	Metres (m)	–
Velocity	Velocity is the rate of change of displacement	Metres per second (m/s)	$\text{velocity} = \dfrac{\text{displacement (m)}}{\text{time taken (s)}}$
Acceleration	Acceleration is the rate of change of velocity	Metres per second squared (m/s^2)	$\text{acceleration} = \dfrac{\text{change in velocity (m/s)}}{\text{time taken (s)}}$
Momentum	Momentum is the product of the mass and velocity of an object	Kilogramme metres per second (kg m/s)	momentum = mass (kg) × velocity (m/s)

Graphs of motion

In your exam you need to be able to plot, label and interpret biomechanical graphs and diagrams, so make sure you understand distance/time graphs and velocity/time graphs.

The relationship between impulse and increasing and decreasing momentum

Impulse is the product of the force applied to an object or a body and the time taken to apply that force. It is calculated as force × time. Using impulse to increase momentum is achieved by increasing the amount of muscular force and the time taken to apply it. Using impulse to decrease momentum is achieved by increasing the time over which forces act upon it. For example, when landing, a gymnast flexes their hips and knees. This extends the time over which the force is applied on the ground and allows them to control the landing.

The interpretation of force/time graphs in sprinting

Impulse is represented by an area under a force/time graph. The graphs in Figure 7 show various stages of a 100 m sprint. In the 100 m sprint, impulse is only concerned with horizontal forces. As the sprinter's foot lands on the ground the muscles contract and a force is applied to the ground (action force) and the ground reaction force then acts on the foot, which allows the athlete to accelerate forwards. The action of the foot in contact with the ground is referred to as a single footfall. It is important to note that, in running/sprinting, negative impulse occurs first when the foot lands to provide a braking action and then positive impulse occurs next as the foot takes off for acceleration.

Exam tip

For graphs of linear motion, always:
- plot time on the horizontal axis
- label the axes, including units in brackets
- use a curved line of best fit

Impulse is force × time and relates to a change in momentum.

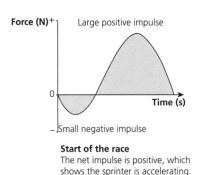

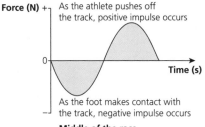

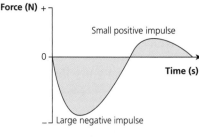

Start of the race
The net impulse is positive, which shows the sprinter is accelerating.

Middle of the race
Both positive and negative impulses are equal (net impulse of zero). This means there is no acceleration or deceleration, so the sprinter is running at a constant velocity.

End of the race
The net impulse is negative, which shows the sprinter is decelerating.

Figure 7 Force/time graphs to show various stages of a 100 m sprint

Summary

After studying this topic you should be able to:
- understand the forces acting on a performer during linear motion
- define the scalars mass, speed and distance and the vectors weight, velocity, displacement, acceleration and momentum, giving equations and units of measurement
- demonstrate the ability to plot, label and interpret biomechanical graphs and diagrams
- explain the relationship between impulse and increasing and decreasing momentum in sprinting through the interpretation of force/time graphs

> **Knowledge check 10**
>
> When does negative impulse occur during sprinting?

Angular motion

Angular motion is movement around a fixed point or axis, for example a somersault, throwing a discus or moving around the high bar in gymnastics.

> **Angular motion** occurs when a force is applied outside the centre of mass (eccentric force).

Application of Newton's laws to angular motion

Just by changing the terminology of Newton's laws we can relate them to angular motion.

Newton's first law: a rotating body will continue in its state of angular motion unless an external rotational force (**torque**) is exerted upon it. An ice skater spinning in the air, for example, will continue to spin until they land. Here the ground exerts an *external force* (torque), which changes their state of angular momentum.

> **Torque** is a rotational force.

Newton's second law: the rate of change of angular momentum of a body is proportional to the force (torque) causing it and the change that takes place in the direction in which the force (torque) acts. Leaning forwards from a diving board, for example, will create more angular momentum than standing straight.

Newton's third law: when a force (torque) is applied by one body to another, the second body will exert an equal and opposite force (torque) on the other body.

For example, performing a twist on the trampoline exerts an equal and opposite force. Pushing down on the trampoline with a right-hand torque will generate an upward and left-hand torque on the trampolinist so they can take off and twist to the left.

Definitions and units for angular motion

Definitions and units for angular motion are outlined in Table 6.

Table 6 Definitions and units for angular motion

Measurement of angular motion	Definition	Units
Angular displacement	The smallest change in angle between the starting and finishing points	radians (1 rad = 57.3 degrees)
Angular velocity	The rotational speed of an object and the axis about which the object is rotating	rad/s $\dfrac{\text{angular displacement (rad)}}{\text{time taken (s)}}$
Angular acceleration	The rate of change of angular velocity over time	rads/s² $\dfrac{\text{change in velocity (rad/s)}}{\text{time taken (s)}}$

Conservation of angular momentum during flight, moment of inertia and its relationship with angular velocity

Moment of inertia is the resistance of a body to angular motion (rotation). This depends upon the mass of the body and the distribution of mass from the axis of rotation. The greater the mass, the greater the resistance to change and therefore the greater the moment of inertia — for example, a medicine ball is more difficult to roll along the ground than a tennis ball. The closer the mass is to the axis of rotation, the easier it is to turn (= low moment of inertia). Increasing the distance of the distribution of mass from the axis of rotation increases the moment of inertia, for example a somersault in a straight position has a higher moment of inertia than the tucked somersault.

Angular momentum is defined by the following equation:

angular momentum (L) = moment of inertia (I) × **angular velocity** (ω)

It is a conserved quantity — it stays constant unless an external force (torque) acts upon it (Newton's first law). When an ice skater executes a spin, for example, there is no change in their angular momentum until they use their blades to slow the spin down. A figure skater can also manipulate their moment of inertia to increase or decrease the speed of the spin (angular velocity). At the start of the spin (Figure 8), the arms and leg are stretched out. This increases their distance from the axis of rotation, resulting in a large moment of inertia and a large angular momentum in order to start the spin (decrease in angular velocity). When the figure skater brings their arms and legs back in line with the rest of his body, the distance of these body parts to the axis of rotation decreases significantly. This reduces the moment of inertia, meaning that angular momentum has to increase (Figure 9). The result is a faster spin (increase in angular velocity).

Knowledge check 11

Explain Newton's second law in relation to a diver performing a double somersault.

Exam tip

Learn the formulae in case you need to do a calculation in your exam. Always show your full workings and the units of measurement to gain some credit even if the final calculation is incorrect.

Moment of inertia is the resistance of a body to change in its state of angular motion or rotation.

Angular momentum is the quantity of angular motion possessed by a body.

Angular velocity refers to the speed and direction of the spin.

Knowledge check 12

Explain the relationship between moment of inertia and angular velocity.

Figure 8 The start of a spin

Figure 9 Increasing angular velocity during a spin

Summary

After studying this topic you should be able to:
- understand and apply Newton's laws to angular motion
- define angular displacement, angular velocity and angular acceleration, and give their units of measurement
- explain the conservation of angular momentum during flight, as well as moment of inertia and its relationship with angular velocity

Projectile motion

Factors affecting horizontal displacement of projectiles

The following factors affect the **horizontal displacement** of a projectile:

- Angle of release — the optimum angle of release is dependent upon release height and landing height. When both the release height and the landing height are equal then the optimum angle of release is 45°. If the release height is below the landing height then the optimum angle of release needs to be greater than 45°. When the release height is greater than the landing height, the optimum angle of release needs to be less than 45°.
- Speed of release — the greater the release velocity of a projectile, the greater the horizontal displacement travelled.
- Height of release — a greater release height also results in an increase in horizontal displacement.

Factors affecting flight paths of different projectiles

Weight (gravity) and air resistance are two forces that affect projectiles while they are in the air. These two factors are crucial in deciding whether a projectile has a flight path that is a true **parabola** or a distorted parabola.

Horizontal displacement is the shortest distance from the starting point to the finishing point in a line parallel to the ground.

Knowledge check 13

What three factors will affect the horizontal displacement of a throw from the boundary line in cricket?

A **parabola** is a uniform curve that is symmetrical at its highest point (i.e. matching left and right sides).

The forces acting on a projectile in flight can be represented with a free-body diagram that shows which forces are acting, where the forces originate, the relative sizes of the forces and the direction in which they are acting on the projectile. This enables us to consider the net force acting on the body and therefore the resulting projectile motion and flight path.

Shot put

Projectiles with a large weight force, such as a shot put, have a small air resistance force and follow a true parabolic flight path.

Figure 10 shows the forces acting on the flight path of a shot put at the start, middle and end of flight. The shot has a large mass, so there is a longer weight arrow (W). The longer the flight path, the more time air resistance (AR) has to affect the projectile and have a greater influence.

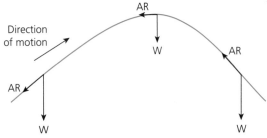

Figure 10 Free-body diagram to show the forces acting an a shot put during flight

Badminton shuttle

For projectiles with a lighter mass, such as a shuttlecock, the effects of air resistance result in a flight path that deviates from a true parabola to a distorted parabola (Figure 11).

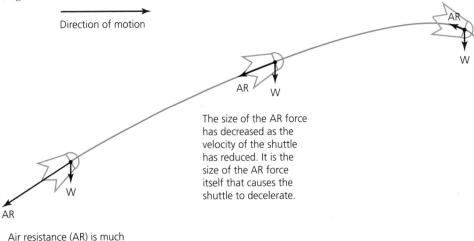

The size of the AR force has decreased as the velocity of the shuttle has reduced. It is the size of the AR force itself that causes the shuttle to decelerate.

The AR force is now small as the velocity of the shuttle has slowed. The weight force has remained the same throughout the flight and is now larger than air resistance. Consequently the shuttle falls vertically, resulting in a non-parabolic flight.

Air resistance (AR) is much larger than weight (W), as the velocity of the shuttle is high as it leaves the racket head.

Figure 11 Free-body diagrams of a shuttlecock in the start-, mid- and end-of-flight phases

Vector components of parabolic flight

A shot put follows a parabolic flight path and because it is released at an angle to the horizontal its initial velocity has a **horizontal component** and a **vertical component**. These two components can be represented by vectors. A vector is drawn as an arrow and it has magnitude (size) and direction. Drawing a bigger arrow means there is more magnitude; a smaller arrow means less magnitude (Figure 12).

No vertical component at the highest flight point

Large positive vertical component on release as the shot put travels up and away from the athlete

Larger negative vertical component before landing due to the effects of gravity

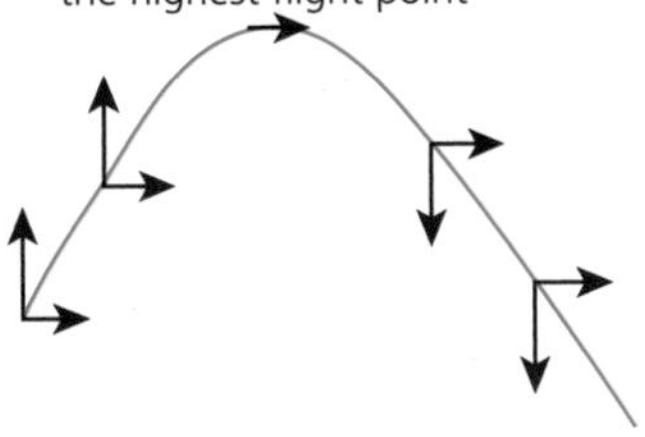

Figure 12 Forces acting on the flight path of a shot put

Here, the vertical component can only be affected by gravity, which is why the vertical component decreases during flight. Air resistance is negligible, so both the horizontal and vertical components are unaffected by air resistance. This means that the horizontal component remains constant throughout the flight.

Horizontal component refers to the horizontal motion of an object.

Vertical component refers to the upward motion of an object.

Exam tip

Make sure you draw the release point of the shot put higher than the landing height.

> **Summary**
>
> After studying this topic you should be able to:
> - identify the angle of release, speed of release and height of release as the factors that affect the horizontal displacement of projectiles
> - explain the factors affecting flight paths of the shot put and shuttlecock
> - identify the vector components of parabolic flight

Fluid mechanics

Dynamic fluid force

Fluid dynamics is the study of fluids and how forces affect them. Drag and lift are dynamic fluid forces.

Drag force

A drag force acts in the opposite direction to motion and therefore has a negative effect on velocity. There are two different types of drag:

- **Surface drag** relates to friction between the surface of an object and the fluid environment. It is sometimes called 'skin drag'. Swimmers wear specialised, smooth clothing and shave off body hair from their arms and torso to reduce surface drag.
- **Form drag** relates to the impact of the fluid environment on an object. It is sometimes referred to as 'shape drag'. The forces affecting the leading edge of an object increase form drag and the forces affecting the trailing edge reduce form drag. Form drag relates to **streamlining**, for example a swimmer has to create the thinnest and straightest form as they move through the water. A large form drag also offers less turbulent air or water for anything that is following, i.e. a slipstream. In cycling, for example, a cyclist will use another rider's slipstream (also known as 'drafting').

Surface drag is the friction between the surface of an object and the fluid environment.

Form drag is the impact of the shape of an object on the fluid environment.

Streamlining involves shaping a body so it can move as effectively and quickly as possible through a fluid.

Factors that reduce and increase drag, and their application to sporting situations

- The greater the velocity of a body through a fluid, the greater the drag force. Consequently, in a sport that is very quick, it is important to reduce the effects of drag. This is done by streamlining and reducing cross-sectional area.
- A large cross-sectional area increases drag. In cycling, competitors reduce their cross-sectional area by crouching low over the handlebars rather than sitting upright.
- A more streamlined, aerodynamic shape reduces drag. A speed skier has a helmet that extends to the shoulders to give them a more streamlined shape. The special form-fitting suit and aerodynamic boots are also streamlined.

The Bernoulli principle applied to sporting situations

For your exam you need to be able to explain the **Bernoulli principle** in relation to the discus, speed skiers, cyclists and racing cars.

Upward lift force

When the discus is thrown, it experiences an upward lift force during flight. This enables it to stay in the air for longer, increasing the horizontal distance it travels. Lift is achieved when different air pressures act on an object. Air that travels faster has a lower pressure than air that travels slower. This is the Bernoulli principle. When a projectile such as the discus is released, the **angle of attack** is important. This changes the flow of air around the discus, so the air that travels over the top of the discus has to travel further than the air underneath. This results in the air above the discus travelling at a faster velocity which creates a lower pressure. This lower pressure above creates an upward lift force, allowing the discus to travel further. If the angle of attack is too great, there is less lift and more drag, causing it to stall.

Downward lift force

The Bernoulli principle can also be used to describe a downward lift force, such as that required by speed skiers, cyclists and racing cars. The skis, bike and car need to be pushed down into the ground so that a greater frictional force is created.

Speed skiers need to stay in contact with the ice for speed as more downward-acting lift means more force, which melts the ice for a more friction-free surface.

In cycling the low streamlined body position over the handlebars, together with the shape of the cyclist's helmet, creates a flat surface, so the air flow over the top of the cyclist travels a shorter distance at a slower velocity than the air underneath. This results in a higher pressure above the cyclist, thus creating a downward lift force which increases friction, allowing the tyres of the bike to maintain a firm grip on the track.

In Formula 1 the car's spoiler is angled so that the lift force can act in a downward direction. This happens because the air that travels over the top of the car travels a shorter distance than the air underneath due to the spoiler angle. As a result the air above travels at a slower velocity and a higher pressure. This creates a downward lift force and more friction, so the tyres maintain a firm grip on the track at high speed.

Knowledge check 14

Identify what is meant by a drag force and, giving an example from sport, explain how the effects of a drag force can be reduced.

The **Bernoulli principle** states that the faster air molecules travel, the less pressure they exert, while the slower they travel, the more pressure they exert.

Angle of attack is the tilt of a projectile relative to the air flow. The angle of attack that produces the best lift for the discus is anything between 25° and 40°.

Knowledge check 15

Explain the Bernoulli principle in relation to a downward lift force for a speed skier.

Exam tip

Remember that the discus has an upward lift force to increase how far it travels, while the racing car, cyclist and speed skier need a downward lift force to maximise speed.

Summary

After studying this topic you should be able to:
- explain the dynamic fluid forces drag and lift
- identify factors that influence drag, and their application to sport
- explain and apply the Bernoulli principle

Sport psychology

Aspects of personality

Personality is the 'unique psychological make-up' of an individual. (Gill)

Psychologists dispute how personality is developed. Some believe that it is natural, while others believe that it is learned. This gives rise to the 'nature vs nurture' debate.

Trait theory

According to trait theory, personality is:

- genetic/natural
- stable/permanent
- enduring
- shown in all situations

For example, a calm, controlled netballer always shows these characteristics even when playing against an opponent who continually makes contact. The coach would be confident that the player would not lash out despite the contact.

Social learning theory

According to social learning theory, personality:

- is learned from our experiences
- is learned by observing and copying significant others
- changes according to the situation
- cannot be predicted
- develops due to socialisation
- is highly likely to be imitated if successful or praised by a coach
- is more likely to be copied if the model shares characteristics such as gender, age or ability level

For example, a tennis coach praises your team-mate for showing determination and controlled emotions during matches. You copy their personality in order to gain the same reinforcement.

Interactionist perspective

This combines both trait and social learning theories. Lewin (1935) suggested that personality is made up of our genetic traits *and* the influence of learning from environmental experiences, i.e. behaviour (B) is a function (f) of an individual's personality traits (P) interacting with the environment (E).

$$B = f(P.E)$$

A performer will adapt to the situation they find themselves in — learning to behave differently from how they normally would. For example, a generally **introverted** rhythmic gymnast might have learned to adapt and now displays more **extroverted** characteristics during a competition in order to appeal to the judges.

Knowledge check 16

Define 'personality'.

Exam tip

If a question asks you about the 'nature vs nurture' debate, ensure that you explain *both* trait and social learning approaches. To really boost your marks, conclude with a statement about the interactionist perspective.

Knowledge check 17

State Lewin's equation to illustrate the interactionist perspective.

An **introvert** has a shy, reserved personality.

An **extrovert** has a sociable, outgoing personality.

According to Hollander (1971), personality can be divided into three levels, as shown in Figure 13.

- **Psychological core** — internal; consistent; stable; the 'real you'; unaffected by the environment/beliefs/values/attitudes. For example, a performer who inherits a low level of aggression is naturally calm.
- **Typical responses** — can be learned; usual responses to environmental situations. For example, an ice hockey player has learned which aggressive acts are acceptable and typically completes highly aggressive tackles.
- **Role-related behaviours** — affected by/fit the environment; superficial; highly changeable. For example, during a semi-final against a local rival, the performer's level of aggressiveness is heightened due to task importance.

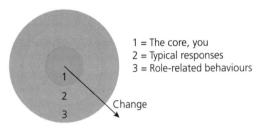

1 = The core, you
2 = Typical responses
3 = Role-related behaviours

Change

Environment

Figure 13 The Hollander model

How knowledge of the interactionist perspective can improve performance

- Identify situations where the performer instinctively responds and use this knowledge to predict behaviour. For example, the coach predicts that the rugby player will respond aggressively to a high tackle. The coach substitutes the player to avoid them being given a red card.
- Create situations in training that cause frustration, for example penalty-talking in front of a crowd. Teach the player cognitive/somatic coping strategies (p. 50).
- Change player behaviour. For example, the coach asks a performer to observe the determination and motivation of their team-mates. If this is then reinforced, the performer is likely to copy.

Exam tip

Trait, social learning and interactionist theories feature in personality, aggression and leadership. Customise practical examples to a specific area of the specification.

Summary

After studying this topic you should be able to:
- clearly define personality
- explain and give examples of the three perspectives of personality

- describe how knowledge of the interactionist perspective can be used to enhance performance

Attitudes

The components of attitudes

The **triadic model** suggests that attitudes are made up of three components:

- **Cognitive** — beliefs/thoughts; for example, I *believe* that attending the gym is good for my physical and mental health.

- **Affective** — emotions/feelings; for example, I *enjoy* attending classes at the gym and feel energised afterwards.
- **Behavioural** — actions/responses; for example, I *attend* the gym five times each week.

Attitude formation

Attitudes can be positive or negative. They are developed through experiences rather than being innate, and often begin to form at an early age.

Social learning involves imitating the attitudes of significant others. If your parents/ friends have a positive attitude towards physical activity, it is likely that you will copy them, especially if you are reinforced or praised for doing so by a coach. High-profile role models in the media often display a positive attitude and, as we regard them highly, we are likely to adopt this positive attitude.

Socialisation occurs when an individual wishes to fit in with the cultural norms surrounding them. If it is the *norm* for your friendship group or family to participate and have positive attitudes towards sport, you will conform in order to fit in. For example, they might all play for a team or attend the gym on a regular basis, and therefore you do the same often because you do not want to feel 'left out'.

Past experiences, for example winning matches or titles, can generate a positive attitude.

Changing attitudes

Cognitive dissonance

When an individual's attitude components match up, whether positively or negatively, they are in a state of cognitive *consonance*. Their beliefs, feelings and actions are in harmony, and their attitude will remain. One way to change an attitude is to create **cognitive dissonance**. Dissonance is caused by generating unease within the individual. This unease is created by changing one or more of the negative attitude components into a positive one, thus causing the individual to question their attitude (Table 7).

Table 7 Ways to create cognitive dissonance by destabilising each attitude component

Negative attitude		Change by
Cognitive	I think that going to the gym is a waste of time	Educating, preferably by a **significant other** Emphasising to them that attending the gym can improve physical and mental health
Affective	I hate going to the gym	Ensuring a positive, varied experience Making it fun/enjoyable Ensuring success
Behavioural	I do not go to the gym	Persuasive communication, preferably by a specialist Praising, which reinforces behaviours, in order to change their attitude towards the gym

Socialisation involves fitting in with cultural norms.

A **significant other** is a person you hold in high esteem/look up to.

Persuasive communication

Persuasive communication is when an individual or group of people encourages you to take on board their point of view so that you have a change in attitude:

- The person trying to persuade should have high status/be significant, and also have good communication skills.
- They should have credibility, i.e. be knowledgeable/proficient/an expert.
- The message should be clear, correct and explicit.
- The person who is listening to the message must understand the information, and ultimately be open to change.
- Peers/other significant people may also be used to support the persuader when giving the message, in order to strengthen their case.

Summary
After studying this topic you should be able to: ■ explain and give examples of each of the attitude components	■ describe how attitudes are formed ■ explain how persuasive communication and cognitive dissonance are used

Exam tip

If a question asks you to describe a positive attitude and your answer refers to negative attitudes (or vice versa) you will not gain credit.

Arousal

Arousal is the level of somatic (body) or cognitive (mind) **stimulation** that gets us ready to perform.

Drive theory

According to **drive theory**, as arousal increases so too does performance quality, so that more drive results in a proportionally increased performance (Figure 14).

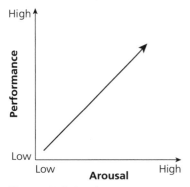

Figure 14 Drive theory

- At high arousal the performer reverts to their **dominant response**. This is a well-learned skill that the performer will use when under competitive pressure.
- If the performer is in the autonomous phase of learning, their dominant response is likely to be correct.
- Cognitive performers are not able to cope with the high level of arousal. Their dominant response is likely to be incorrect.
- Performance is a function of drive multiplied by habit:

$$P = f(D \times H)$$

A **dominant response** is a well-learned skill that the performer will revert to when under competitive pressure.

Exam tip

When describing drive theory, ensure that you refer to both the theoretical equation and the dominant response.

Inverted U theory

The inverted U theory accounts for how different personality types, performers and skills, can be successful.

As arousal increases, so too does performance quality, up to an optimum point at moderate arousal. As it increases further, performance quality decreases as a result of over-arousal.

Under- and over-arousal result in lower performance quality.

Modifications to the inverted U theory

Figure 15 shows how the task and the performer can affect the optimal level of arousal for best performance.

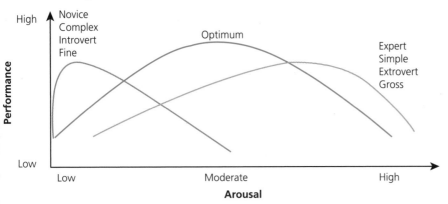

Figure 15 Adaptations to the inverted U theory

The green curve represents optimum performance occurring at lower levels of arousal. This is associated with:

- cognitive performers
- fine skills, requiring a high level of precision and control
- complex skills, where several decisions are made
- introverts, who have a highly stimulated reticular activating system (RAS)

The blue curve represents optimum performance occurring at higher levels of arousal, because additional stimulation can be tolerated. This is associated with:

- autonomous performers
- gross skills, where precision and control are not needed
- simple skills, with few decisions to make
- extroverts, whose RAS experiences low stimulation and who strive for 'exciting' situations

Catastrophe theory

Catastrophe theory (Figure 16) accounts for the sudden drop in performance once the optimum has been exceeded.

- It is multidimensional, considering the effects of both cognitive and somatic anxiety.
- As arousal increases so does performance quality up to an optimum point, at moderate arousal, as shown by the inverted U theory.
- There is then a dramatic decrease in performance as a result of high cognitive anxiety combined with high somatic anxiety.

- The body and the mind have become over-aroused, causing an immediate decline in performance.
- The effects can be reversed by performing relaxation techniques, such as deep breathing exercises/PMR.

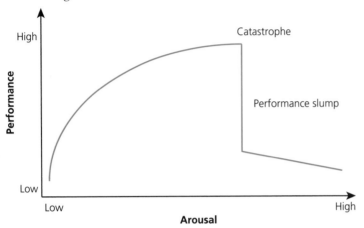

Figure 16 Catastrophe theory

Zone of optimum functioning

The zone of optimum functioning (Figure 17) is a mental state that performers normally only experience once or twice in their entire sporting career, when everything is 'perfect'.

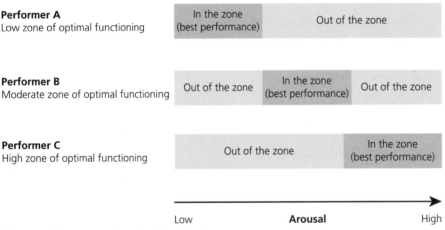

Figure 17 The zone of optimal functioning

Characteristics of 'the zone' include:

- feeling completely calm
- complete control — fully concentrated on the task
- performing on 'autopilot' — some performers have no memory of it
- complete confidence — success is inevitable
- fluent, smooth, efficient performance

Hanin suggests that optimum performance is reached during a band or zone, not at a point (as described by the inverted U theory). Performer A in Figure 17 enters the zone, achieving best performance, at low levels of arousal. Performer B is in the zone at moderate levels of arousal. Performer C enters the zone at high levels of arousal.

Peak flow experience

Peak flow describes the positive psychological state of a performer when they have:
- a challenge to match their skill level
- a clear goal
- the correct attentional style
- a positive attitude before and during the performance
- controlled arousal levels

To achieve peak flow performers should be given a task that is realistic yet challenging. They can then enter the zone.

Summary

After studying this topic you should be able to:
- describe and give practical examples of each of the theories of arousal
- describe what it is like to 'be in the zone'
- describe what it is like to experience peak flow

Anxiety

Anxiety negatively effects performance because the performer experiences worry, nervousness and apprehension.

Types of anxiety

- **Somatic anxiety** — physiological symptoms, for example increased heart rate, sweat levels and muscle tension.
- **Cognitive anxiety** — mental symptoms, for example worrying, irrational thoughts and learned helplessness (p. 43).
- **Competitive trait anxiety** — experiencing nervousness in all competitions regardless of type of event, for example worrying and sweating before every match.
- **Competitive state anxiety** — experiencing nervousness in certain competitions/ certain aspects of the event only, for example only thinking irrational thoughts when taking a penalty, or having high blood pressure during finals only.

Measuring anxiety

Observation
- Real-life method/realistic.
- Anxiety can be analysed before, during and after play.
- Can be used in training.
- **Subjective**/not objective.
- Need to know how the performer acts 'normally'.
- May require several observers.
- Can be time consuming.
- Performers act differently when they know they are being observed.

Knowledge check 20

What is the difference between cognitive and somatic anxiety?

Subjective information is based on the person's opinion.

Questionnaires

- Performer answers a series of questions about their emotions in different situations.
- Quick, cheap and efficient.
- Deal with a lot of data.
- Large numbers of players can be assessed in a short period of time.
- Results are easily compared.
- Socially desirable answers may be given instead of being truthful.
- Performers may not understand the questions.
- The answers given may be affected by mood.
- Examples include the Sports Competition Anxiety Test (SCAT) and the Competitive State Anxiety Inventory 2 (CSAI-2).

Physiological tests

- Generate factual data on physiological responses, for example heart rate/sweat levels.
- Objective.
- Results can be compared easily.
- Used in training and fixtures.
- Performers wear monitors that may become restrictive.
- Performers become more nervous if playing while wearing a heart rate monitor, giving incorrect readings.
- Cost of equipment can be high.

> **Exam tip**
>
> Extended questions often ask you to explain how to control anxiety/stress. Ensure that you include both somatic and cognitive strategies in your answer, and always relate to sporting situations.

Summary

After studying this topic you should be able to:
- explain and give examples of the four types of anxiety
- give advantages and disadvantages of the three ways of measuring anxiety

Aggression

Aggression is:
- the intent to harm
- outside the rules
- reactive
- out of control
- deliberate/hostile

For example, a rugby league player angrily punching his opponent when getting up to play the ball.

> **Aggression** involves intent to harm and is outside of the rules.

Assertion is:
- within the rules
- not intended to harm
- well motivated
- goal directed

For example, a crunching but fair tackle in rugby union.

> **Assertion** involves hard but fair play.

Theories of aggression

Instinct theory

- There is a natural trait or predisposition to be aggressive.
- It is genetic — we are born with a natural tendency to defend ourselves/our territory.
- Aggression inevitably builds up.
- With enough provocation, we will respond aggressively.
- Once the act is complete, we experience catharsis (a release of emotions).
- For example, a wicketkeeper continually sledges a batsman in cricket. Eventually the batsman retaliates and pushes the wicketkeeper.

Knowledge check 21

What is catharsis?

Frustration–aggression hypothesis

- The performer has a drive to achieve a goal (e.g. a basketball player dribbling towards the basket to score).
- The goal is blocked (the defender fouls the player).
- Frustration is experienced, which leads inevitably to aggression (the player feels frustrated and hits out at the defender).
- The release of aggression leads to catharsis (the player feels better and continues to play once the aggression has been released).
- Alternatively the aggression is punished, leading to further frustration and therefore aggression (the official calls a foul and turns the ball over; the player feels even more frustrated and commits an illegal tackle on an opponent).

Aggressive cue theory

- The performer's goal is blocked.
- Arousal levels increase, leading to frustration.
- The performer is now *ready* for an aggressive act, rather than experiencing inevitable aggression.
- An aggressive act is more likely to occur if learned cues/triggers are present.
- If the cues/triggers are not present, an aggressive act is less likely.
- For example, potentially aggressive objects, such as bats/clubs, or aggressive contact sports, such as rugby/ice hockey, are more likely to produce aggressive responses. A footballer who has been praised by their coach for aggressive, dangerous tackles, may learn that this is a positive behaviour and therefore in future matches the coach acts as a cue to be aggressive.

Social learning theory

- This opposes the trait approach.
- It is based on the work of Bandura.
- Individuals learn aggression by watching and copying significant others.
- Reinforced/successful actions are more likely to be copied.
- Socialisation is important.
- Aggression is more likely to be copied if the model shares similar characteristics.
- For example, a young rugby player watches their idol perform a high tackle on an opponent. The crowd cheers and the opponent is prevented from scoring a try. Because this aggressive act is reinforced and successful, the young player copies this behaviour in their next match.

Exam tip

In 'theories of aggression' questions, ensure that you state the name of each theory clearly and write about all four.

Strategies to control aggression

Table 8 Strategies to control aggression that can be utilised by players and/or coaches

Players	Coaches
Cognitive techniques: ■ mental rehearsal ■ imagery ■ visualisation ■ selective attention ■ negative thought stopping ■ positive self-talk Somatic techniques: ■ progressive muscular relaxation ■ breathing control ■ centring ■ biofeedback	Praise non-aggressive acts Highlight non-aggressive role models Punish aggression, for example using substitution/fines Set process and performance goals rather than outcome goals Ensure their own behaviour is not aggressive Give the performer responsibility within the team, for example captaincy

Summary

After studying this topic you should be able to:
■ clearly distinguish between aggression and assertion
■ explain and give examples to illustrate the four theories of aggression
■ describe a range of strategies to control aggression

Exam tip

To access all the marks available on a question about reducing/controlling aggression, give a range of strategies — cognitive, somatic, player and coach.

Motivation

Motivation is a person's desire to succeed. It is an individual's drive that inspires them to perform in sport.

Intrinsic motivation

■ This comes from within the performers themselves.
■ They participate for the 'love' of the sport/pride in achieving their own goals.
■ Performers maintain participation for a longer period of time than when using extrinsic methods.

Extrinsic motivation

■ This comes from an outside source.
■ Tangible, physical rewards include money and trophies.
■ Intangible, non-physical rewards include praise from the coach or crowd.
■ It attracts performers to the sport.
■ It is useful for cognitive performers.
■ It raises confidence.

Knowledge check 22

What is the difference between tangible and intangible rewards?

Summary

After studying this topic you should be able to:
■ give a clear definition of motivation
■ define and give examples of the four types of motivation

Exam tip

Do not refer to internal and external. Use the correct terms — intrinsic and extrinsic.

Achievement motivation theory

Characteristics of achievement motivation

Atkinson and McClelland suggested that in demanding situations performers will exhibit either NACH (need to achieve) or NAF (need to avoid failure) characteristics (Table 9). This is based on their personality and the situational factors, and dictates the level of competitiveness shown.

Knowledge check 23

What types of behaviour do NACH and NAF performers exhibit?

Table 9 Characteristics of NACH and NAF performers

NACH performer	NAF performer
Exhibits approach behaviour	Exhibits avoidance behaviour
Has high self-efficacy/confidence	Has low self-efficacy/confidence
Enjoys challenges	Dislikes challenges
Takes risks	Will take the easy option
Is task persistent	Gives in easily, especially if failing
Regards failure as a step to success	Does not welcome feedback
Uses feedback as a way to improve	May experience learned helplessness
Takes personal responsibility for the outcome	Attributes failure internally
Attributes success internally	Is not competitive — likes tasks with:
Is very competitive — likes tasks with:	■ a high probability of success, i.e. an easy task
■ a low **probability of success**, i.e. a challenging task	■ a low incentive value, i.e. little satisfaction in achieving their goal
■ a high **incentive value**, i.e. will be extremely proud to have achieved their goal	For example, a mid-table squash player prefers to play opponents from the bottom of the table rather than those near to them in ranking because they are highly likely to win
For example, a snowboarder takes the risky black off-piste route rather than the easier blue run down the mountain, knowing that they are likely to fall over, but sees it as a challenge	

Exam tip

When describing NACH and/or NAF performers, include personality and situational components in your answer.

Probability of success is the likelihood of completing the task successfully.

Incentive value is the worth placed on completing the task.

Achievement goal theory

Three factors interact to determine the performer's motivation:

■ The type of achievement goals set:
- Outcome goals focus on defeating others.
- Task goals focus on improving performance from last time.
■ How the performer views success and failure:
- Outcome-oriented performers view success as being shown to be superior to others. They give external attributions, such as poor luck when failing, and exhibit low effort. They dislike evaluative situations.
- Task-oriented performers set difficult tasks, do not fear failure and the perception of their *own* ability relates to their *own* performances rather than their opponent's. They offer internal and unstable attributions.
■ The performer's perceived ability:
- Outcome-oriented performers perceive their ability as high when they win and low when they lose.

– Task-oriented performers focus on improving relative to themselves and therefore their perceived ability is enhanced by feelings of enjoyment, satisfaction and mastery.

In order to generate a NACH approach:

- Ensure success by setting achievable process and performance/task-orientated goals.
- Raise confidence by giving positive reinforcement.
- Highlight successful role models who have comparable characteristics.
- Use attribution retraining.
- Credit internal reasons for success, for example ability to succeed.

Summary

After studying this topic you should be able to:
- describe the personality and situational components of achievement motivation in relation to NACH and NAF performers
- describe outcome- and task-orientated goals
- explain ways to develop NACH approach behaviours

Social facilitation

Social facilitation and inhibition

Performers react differently to being observed while participating. Some enjoy performing with an audience and as a result their performance improves. This is **social facilitation**. However, some people dislike performing with an audience and their performance worsens when being observed. This is **social inhibition**.

Zajonc suggested that four types of 'others' can be present during performance (Figure 18).

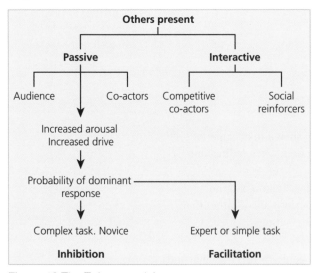

Figure 18 The Zajonc model

Knowledge check 24

What is the difference between social facilitation and social inhibition?

Exam tip

Ensure you know and can explain all aspects of Zajonc's model. The model will not always be given to you. If it does not appear in the question, draw and fully label it because it will help you to structure your answer.

Passive others do not interact with the performer, but by being present they have an effect. They include:

- the audience — observers who do not speak, but just watch, for example the silent observers during a tee-off in golf or a scout turning up unannounced. Their presence makes you feel anxious and can affect your performance.
- co-actors, who are performing the same task, at the same time, but are not competing against you. For example, seeing another cyclist in front of you makes you speed up to overtake them. You win nothing by doing so, but their presence makes you cycle faster.

Interactive others communicate directly with the performer. They include:

- competitive co-actors — the opposition, for example other swimmers in a race, who are in direct rivalry with you
- social reinforcers/supporters — the coach/crowd, for example the spectators at a rugby match cheer or shout at performers

When others are present, the main effect is increased arousal, causing the performer to revert to using their dominant response (see drive theory, p. 28). They may also experience evaluation apprehension.

Social facilitation is likely to occur when:

- the performer is **autonomous** — their skills are grooved and they are used to performing in front of an audience
- performing a **gross skill** — large muscle group movements that do not require precision/accuracy
- performing a **simple skill** — requiring limited decision making/information processing
- the performer is an **extrovert** — they seek social situations and have low levels of natural arousal, meaning that their RAS is activated only with high levels of stimulation. They see the presence of the audience as an opportunity to 'show off' and rise to the challenge.

Social inhibition is likely to occur when:

- the performer is **cognitive** — their skills are performed with limited success and they find performing in front of an audience intimidating
- performing a **fine skill** — requiring precision and accuracy, which is difficult to maintain during high arousal
- performing a **complex skill** — requiring several decisions to be made and lots of information processing, which may not be performed successfully during high arousal
- the performer is an **introvert** — they dislike social situations and have high levels of natural arousal, meaning that their RAS is activated with low levels of stimulation. They find performing in front of others demanding, and this has a detrimental effect on their performance.

Evaluation apprehension

Evaluation apprehension is the fear of being judged and it causes the performer to revert back to their dominant response. The performer may not be being judged, but

> **Exam tip**
>
> To understand social facilitation you will also need a solid understanding of arousal, particularly drive theory.

> **Evaluation apprehension** is the fear of being judged.

if they *perceive* that they are then this will have an effect on their performance. Other factors causing evaluation apprehension include the following:

- If the audience is knowledgeable the performer will be more nervous, for example when a scout is watching.
- If significant others, such as parents/peers, are present.
- If the audience is supportive/abusive, the performance will be facilitated/inhibited.
- If the performer naturally has high trait anxiety, they will be inhibited by an audience
- If the performer has low self-efficacy and therefore does not believe in their ability, they will be inhibited.

Strategies to eliminate the effects of social inhibition

- Familiarisation training — allowing an audience to watch or playing crowd noise while you are training.
- Increasing self-efficacy.
- Practising skills until they are grooved.
- Selective attention — blocking out the crowd and concentrating on the relevant stimuli, such as the ball/opposition.
- Mental rehearsal — going over the performance in your mind to maintain focus and lower arousal levels.
- Using imagery and positive self-talk, and stopping negative thoughts.
- In addition, the coach could:
  - decrease the importance of the task
  - offer encouragement, positive reinforcement and praise to the performer in order to support them

Summary

After studying this topic you should be able to:
- describe social facilitation and social inhibition
- define evaluation apprehension and explain the causes
- describe strategies to eliminate the effects of social inhibition

Group dynamics

Group dynamics is the study of groups, group members and how they operate. A group is *two or more* people who:

- interact/communicate with each other
- share a common goal — they have the same aim
- have mutual awareness — they influence and depend on each other

Tuckman suggested that in order to become a group, members go through four key stages: forming, storming, norming and performing (Table 10).

Table 10 Tuckman's team formation model

Forming	Storming	Norming	Performing
Working out if they belong with the group Learning about other members/coaches Developing social relationships Figuring out the goal Reliant on the coach to bring the group closer For example, during your first training sessions you decide that you want to be part of the hockey team as they seem to share your passion to win; you begin to socialise with other team members	Infighting and conflict Teams often fold Confrontation with the leaders Members actively challenge for their role/position Self-preservation is important For example, both you and another team member wish to be the goalkeeper, which causes rivalry between you; you also believe that the captain is weak, and that you could do a better job	Conflicts resolved Group cohesion develops; members become unified Norms are set Members cooperate to achieve potential Motivation and success levels rise For example, you decide that your team-mate is an effective goalkeeper and that you can use your skills in an outfield position, giving the team an excellent defence; you respect the captain and are aware of their qualities	Group stabilised All concentrate on the group succeeding Motivation and enjoyment levels are high Respect for other members and leaders is high For example, your team plays regularly and members praise each other for team success, which is increasing because the team is now functioning as a unit

Group cohesion

A **cohesive** team has unity, a structure, and all pull together in order to reach their shared aim. The more cohesive a team is the more successful it will be. Group cohesion takes two forms:

- **Task cohesion** — members work in unity to achieve their potential and meet the common aim. They may not socialise together. This is important in interactive sports, such as football and volleyball, where the team members must work together and rely on each other's timing and coordination.
- **Social cohesion** — members get along and feel attached to others. They communicate with and support each other inside and outside of the sporting arena. This is important in more co-active sports, where your individual effort contributes to a whole team performance, for example a swimming relay team.

By raising cohesiveness and reducing faulty processes such as **social loafing** within a team, the coach can improve individual and whole-team performance. The more an individual feels part of, and valued within, a team the more likely it is they will succeed.

Steiner's model

According to Steiner:

actual productivity = potential productivity – losses due to faulty processes

Actual productivity is the team's level of achievement on a specific task, for example the team reached the semi-final of a cup competition.

Potential productivity is the team's best possible level of achievement when it is cohesive, for example the team could have won the cup competition.

Losses due to faulty processes are the coordination and cooperation problems the team faced, which reduced the level of cohesion and therefore lowered its level of achievement. For example, some team members lacked the motivation to attend

Exam tip

When describing group cohesion, refer to task and social cohesion in your answer.

Social loafing involves reducing effort/'hiding' when in a team. See also p. 40.

Knowledge check 25

State the equation that describes Steiner's model of productivity.

training so the team could not fully practice set plays, impacting negatively on coordination.

Potential productivity

This refers to the level an individual/team can achieve when performing at its best. Steiner suggested that teams face many problems that affect their productivity, including:

- coordination problems — team members failing to communicate properly with each other, resulting in poor timing/set plays breaking down
- members lacking understanding of their role in the team
- members lacking understanding of tactics or strategies set by the coach
- motivation losses, such as team members withdrawing effort when training and/or competing
- the Ringlemann effect and social loafing (see below)

The Ringlemann effect and social loafing

The Ringlemann effect and social loafing are both faulty processes, which have a detrimental effect on the cohesiveness and attainment of a team. Long-term effects include performers withdrawing from and/or avoiding sporting activity altogether.

The **Ringlemann effect** was suggested after a 'tug-of-war' experiment showed that eight participants failed to pull eight times as hard as a single participant. Ringlemann's study found that as the number of people in the group increased, the level of performance of individuals in the group decreased. For example, a rugby union player performs much better when playing in a seven-a-side tournament than when playing in a full fifteen-a-side game. It was suggested that the reduction in performance in the tug-of-war was due to the lack of coordination, i.e. they were not all pulling on the rope in unison. However, later studies showed that a reduction in motivation was the cause rather than a loss of coordination.

Social loafing is when a performer lowers the level of effort they contribute to the team. This happens when they believe that they are not valued, and their input is going unnoticed, so they stop trying. If you have played well but never received praise from the coach, you will eventually give up. Other factors causing performers to loaf include:

- no clear role within group (e.g. unsure of position within team)
- low self-efficacy/confidence
- learned helplessness
- team-mates not trying, so you also stop putting in effort (e.g. your winger fails to chase a ball, which goes into touch, so you question why you should bother)
- the coach/captain being a poor leader — they do not encourage you and/or use weak strategies
- high levels of trait/state anxiety
- injury (e.g. you twisted an ankle in training and therefore you decide not to bother reaching to return wide serves in tennis)
- social inhibition as a result of an offensive crowd

Exam tip

Remember to use the correct terminology when referring to Tuckman's and Steiner's models to access the marks.

Strategies to improve cohesion and overcome social loafing, in order to enhance team performance include:

- highlighting individual performances (e.g. by giving statistics — shots on target, tackles, assists etc.)
- giving specific roles/responsibility within the team
- developing social cohesion (e.g. team-building exercises, tours)
- rewarding cohesive behaviour (e.g. praising effective teamwork)
- raising individuals' confidence
- encouraging group identity (e.g. having a set kit)
- effective leadership that matches the preferred style of the group
- selecting players who work well together, rather than individual 'stars'
- setting achievable process/performance goals rather than outcome goals
- continually emphasising the team goal
- selecting players who do not socially loaf
- punishing social loafing
- grooving set plays/complete coordination practice

Summary

After studying this topic you should be able to:

- explain how groups are formed according to Tuckman's model
- describe and give examples of task and social cohesion
- explain and give examples of Steiner's model
- describe the Ringelmann effect and social loafing
- explain strategies to improve cohesion and reduce social loafing

Importance of goal setting

Benefits of goal setting

Psychological research shows that setting goals has positive effects on performance, including:

- giving the performer an aim or focus
- increasing motivation when the goal is accomplished
- increasing confidence levels
- controlling arousal/anxiety levels
- increasing commitment
- maintaining **task persistence**
- focusing efforts on training and game situations

Task persistence involves persevering with efforts to achieve a goal.

Types of goal

Process goals — relatively short-term goals set to improve technique, for example an ice dancer aims to improve their toe loop technique.

Performance goals — intermediate goals often set against yourself to improve performance from last time, for example aiming to score more points than in the last competition.

Outcome goals — long-term goals reached after extensive work, often set against others to win, for example aiming to win the county ice dance championships.

Principles of effective goal setting

When setting goals, the SMARTER principles should be followed (Table 11).

Table 11 The SMARTER principles

Principle	Explanation	Example
Specific	The goal must be exact, clear and precise so that the performer knows what to aim for; it should relate to the performer's role	Netball goal attack to score 90% of goals
Measurable	The goal must be quantifiable, so progress can be monitored	Aim to reduce 400 m time by 2 seconds by end of season
Achievable	The performer must have the ability to complete the task so that motivation is maintained	Coach sets a relatively experienced runner the target of running 10 km in under 60 minutes because they both believe that it is possible
Realistic	It must be challenging but within the performer's reach in order to motivate and sustain effort; if it is too difficult, it may cause anxiety	Novice skier aims to complete a blue run without falling over during their first ever week of skiing
Time-bound	A set period must be established to monitor progress and assess if the goal has been met	Perform a PB time in the 100 m freestyle by the end of next month
Evaluate	The performer and coach should review how and when the goal was achieved, and consider the effectiveness of the methods used	Performer and coach review the timeline and training methods used to meet the target of jumping a PB in the long jump; successful methods will be used in the future
Re-do	If the goal is not met or significant progress is not made, the target should be adjusted to help the performer to succeed	Rugby player is unable to reach his target of 50% completed tackles each match; his target is adjusted to 45% to enable him to succeed, which increases his motivation and confidence

Summary

After studying this topic you should be able to:
- explain the benefits of setting the various types of goal
- describe the SMARTER principles of goal setting

Attribution theory

Attribution theory tells us how individuals explain their behaviour. In sport, performers use attributions to offer reasons for why they have won or lost.

Weiner's model

Weiner's model illustrates the following:
- The **locus of causality** — *where* the performer places the reason for the win/loss:
  - **Internal** — within the performer's control, for example the natural *ability* they possess or the *effort* put into training.
  - **External** — out of the performer's control/controlled by the environment, for example *task difficulty* (strength of opposition faced) or *luck* (decisions made by officials or environmental factors, e.g. an unlucky ball bounce).

Knowledge check 26

Name the three types of goal.

Exam tip

You must say why the SMARTER principle is used, for example being measurable allows progress to be tracked.

Knowledge check 27

What is an attribution?

- The **stability dimension** — how *fixed/changeable* the attributions are:
  - **Stable** — relatively permanent, for example the *ability* (internal, stable) of the performer remains the same over time; *task difficulty* (external, stable), for example the ability of the opposition.
  - **Unstable**/very changeable — changes from week to week or even within minutes in a fixture, for example the *effort* (internal, unstable) is higher when chasing down a ball at the start of the match when taking the lead, than towards the end of the same match when losing; *luck* (external, unstable) is very changeable, for example if the tennis ball hits the top of the net, whether it bounces on your side or the opposition's side is down to luck.

Weiner suggested that attributions can be classified as shown in Table 12.

Table 12 Weiner's attribution model

		The locus of causality	
		Internal	External
Stability dimension	Stable	Ability	Task difficulty
	Unstable	Effort	Luck

Self-serving bias, attribution retraining and learned helplessness

Self-serving bias is using external and/or unstable reasons for losing, and internal reasons for success.

- To keep performers motivated and sustain confidence, attribute losing to external reasons or to unstable/changeable factors, i.e. state that task difficulty/luck/low effort were the reasons for the loss.
- Highlight effort, and suggest that with increased effort results can be changed.
- Avoid suggesting that losing is due to internal/stable reasons, because this can reduce motivation and cause **learned helplessness**.

Learned helplessness develops when performers attribute failure internally to stable reasons, for example 'I lost the swimming race because I simply do not have the ability.' They believe that no matter what they do or how hard they try, they are destined to fail and therefore are not task persistent. This can be either general, relating to all sports (e.g. 'I can't succeed in any sport') or specific, relating to one skill in sport (e.g. 'I can't take penalty flicks in hockey because I will miss') or a single sport (e.g. 'I can't play badminton').

In order to reduce the effects of learned helplessness, the performer should change their negative attributions into positive ones, a process known as **attribution retraining**. Both performers and coaches alike should always attribute the reasons for winning internally to ability and effort (rather than externally to luck), while those for failure should be attributed externally rather than internally to ability. When coaches and players use correct attributions, motivation will be sustained and performers will increase their task persistence. This also helps to avoid learned helplessness.

Learned helplessness is the feeling that failure is inevitable. It can be global or specific.

Exam tip

Questions may ask you to describe learned helplessness. Include general and specific examples in your answer.

Strategies to avoid learned helplessness

- Set realistic process and/or performance goals that enable the performer to succeed.
- Raise self-efficacy.
- Highlight previous high-quality performances.
- Give positive reinforcement and encouragement to raise confidence.
- Give demonstrations that are within the player's capability.
- Use cognitive and somatic stress management techniques, such as imagery or centring.

Summary

After studying this topic you should be able to:
- describe the attribution process
- explain Weiner's model and link each part to a sporting example
- describe the link between attribution, task persistence and motivation
- define self-serving bias, attribution retraining and learned helplessness
- describe strategies for avoiding learned helplessness

Self-efficacy and confidence

Characteristics of self-efficacy, self-confidence and self-esteem

Self-efficacy is how much belief you have in your ability to achieve a goal. It is the belief you have that you can be successful when carrying out a specific task.

Self-confidence is a generalised feeling of assurance that you have the ability to meet demands — an absence of doubt.

Self-esteem is how much value you think you have — how positively you regard yourself.

Bandura's self-efficacy theory

Self-efficacy relates to the amount of confidence you have in a particular sporting situation. It is specific rather than general, and varies in different circumstances.

Bandura suggested that four factors can influence the level of self-efficacy shown by a performer. By raising their efficacy levels in one situation to begin with, coaches can increase the performer's self-esteem and belief in their ability to master other tasks. For example, a young gymnast experiences fear when performing on a full-height beam. To increase her self-efficacy, the coach should use the four factors shown in Table 13.

Table 13 Bandura's four sources of self-efficacy

Performance accomplishments	Vicarious experiences	Verbal persuasion	Emotional arousal
Remind performers of past success in similar situations For example, remind the gymnast that she was brilliant on the lower beam and that she did not fall off	Use a role model who shares characteristics with the performer (e.g. ability, gender, age) to show that it is possible for them to achieve also For example, ask a gymnast of similar age and standard to perform on the beam; the young gymnast will think 'if they can do it, so can I!'	Encourage the performer and tell them that they believe they can succeed To enhance this, significant others should be used For example, the coach and friends of the gymnast could persuade her that they believe she can perform well on the beam	Often performers notice that they have become over aroused due to the obvious psychological and physiological symptoms (e.g. increased heart rate and sweating) This reduces their self-efficacy because they *perceive* that they are unable to meet the demands of the task In order to control arousal, show the performer how to use cognitive and somatic management strategies For example, the coach tells the performer to use mental rehearsal to go over the moves on the beam in her mind before mounting; this will allow her to focus and will lower her arousal level

Vealey's model of sports confidence

Athletes who have high confidence in one sporting situation will feel more confident in their ability to succeed in others. To raise confidence levels, performers should experience success.

Vealey suggested that the performer will judge their ability to succeed in a task (e.g. taking a conversion in rugby) with a certain amount of each of the following:

- **Trait sport confidence (SC-trait)** — their natural, innate confidence level, for example they are a generally confident performer, so believe that they can succeed in sport.
- **State sport confidence (SC-state)** — their level of confidence in this situation (self-efficacy) is often based on past experiences, for example they assume that they will score because they have kicked many conversions before.
- **Competive orientation** — how competitive the performer is and the types of goals they may have set themselves. For example, the kicker is very driven and has set himself the performance goal of kicking 90% of his attempts.

The three factors above combine to give the performer a level of confidence in the objective sporting situation (Figure 19).

Knowledge check 28

Name the four sources of self-efficacy in Bandura's model.

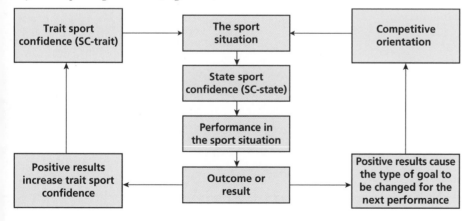

Figure 19 Vealey's model of sports confidence

The performer produces the response, for example attempts the conversion, and considers the **subjective outcomes**. If they judge the outcome as being a positive result, for example they successfully kick the conversion, then the level of general SC-trait and specific SC-state will *increase*. This will further the chances of approach behaviour being shown in other sporting situations. A successful attempt will also increase the level of competitive orientation shown by the performer, for example the kicker becomes even more motivated and sets a new goal of 95% success rate.

Knowledge check 29

According to Vealey, what is SC-trait?

Exam tip

In answers relating to Bandura's/Vealey's models, keep the same example throughout and refer to the skill at each stage.

Effects of home field advantage

Performers usually perform better/win more games when playing at home. Home fixtures normally mean that there is a large number of supporters present (see social facilitation, p. 36), and the home team is familiar with the venue, keeping uncertainty and arousal levels low. This results in improved confidence and motivation. If the audience is very close to the playing area, home-field advantage is even more important, for example on a basketball court. However, during the later stages of a competition, the pressure may be extremely high due to the home crowd expectations of winning, resulting in social inhibition.

Summary

After studying this topic you should be able to:
- define self-confidence, self-efficacy and self-esteem
- explain and give examples of Bandura's and Vealey's models
- describe strategies to develop self-efficacy
- describe the effects of home field advantage

Leadership

Effective leaders:
- have a clear vision or goal
- have effective communication skills
- are ambitious
- are motivators/motivated
- are charismatic
- are knowledgeable about the sport/skilful
- are empathetic
- are confident
- are adaptable

Styles of leadership

There is a range of styles that a leader may choose to use, as shown in Table 14.

Table 14 Styles of leadership

Autocratic/task-orientated	Democratic/socially orientated	Laissez-faire
Dictatorial in style Focused on ensuring that the task is fulfilled Sole decision maker Used in dangerous situations Used with large groups Used if time is limited Used with hostile groups Used with cognitive performers Preferred by male performers	Focused on ensuring that relationships are developed within the group Group members are involved in making decisions Used with small groups Used if lots of time available Used with friendly groups Used with advanced performers Preferred by female performers	The leader is more of a 'figurehead' than an active leader Group members make all of the decisions Useful if a problem-solving approach is required Only effective with advanced performers

Prescribed leaders are chosen from outside the group, for example the national governing bodies appoint national team managers. They often bring new ideas to the group, but can cause disagreements if the group members are opposed to the appointment.

Emergent leaders are selected from within the group, often because they are nominated by the other group members, for example a Sunday league football team might vote the previous season's 'player's player' as their new captain. There is already a high level of respect for this person, but because they have had the same experiences as the other team members, they may not be able to bring any new strategies to enable the team to progress.

Knowledge check 30

Name the three styles of leadership.

Theories of leadership in different sporting situations

Fiedler's contingency model

Fiedler suggested an interactionist approach in which an effective leader will match their style with the situation they are faced with. One of two leadership styles should be adopted:

- A task-orientated leader is mainly concerned with achieving the goals that are set and takes a pragmatic approach to get thing done. They are very direct and authoritarian. This style should be used in the most and least favourable situations.
- A person-orientated leader focuses on developing harmony and good relationships within the group. They are open to suggestions and take more of a democratic approach. This style should be used in moderately favourable situations.

In the most favourable situations, the leader is in a strong position of authority and has the respect of the group, i.e. the members have good relationships with each other and the task is clear. For example, a team who have played together for a number of years under the same captain and who have good relationships with one another may have a number of set plays rehearsed. When the captain calls the play, they are all aware of what should happen and complete the move immediately. In this situation, a task-orientated approach would work best to complete the task effectively.

In the least favourable situations, the leader has no power or respect from the group, there may be infighting in the group and hostility towards the leader, with the task being unclear. For example, a supply teacher is asked to take a year 9 PE class. They do not know the students, the group may not show them any respect and they are unclear as to what activities to teach. In this situation a task-orientated approach would also need to be used in order to motivate the students and to ensure an activity could run in that lesson.

Task-orientated leadership should also be used with cognitive performers, large groups, when time is limited and in dangerous situations.

In moderately favourable situations, the leader would choose a person-orientated style, which allows other team members to contribute to the decision-making process. The leader would have some power/respect, some good relationships and parts of the task would be clear. For example, two new players join your netball team. The whole team offers opinions as to which positions are best for them.

Person-orientated leadership should also be used with advanced performers, smaller groups, with large amounts of time or when tasks are not dangerous.

Chelladurai's multi-dimensional model

Chelladurai's model suggests the leader must be able to **adapt**. They must consider three factors before leading the group:

- **Situation** — this includes the strength of the opponents or if there is any danger involved, for example learning to trampoline is dangerous and requires an autocratic approach.
- **Leader** — this includes their ability, personality and preferred leadership style, for example if the leader is highly experienced, they may prefer to use an autocratic style.
- **Group** — this includes their ability levels and the relationships with each other and with the leader, for example the group might be cognitive performers, and therefore need to be given direct instructions about how to perform moves on the trampoline bed.

Leadership style is also affected by the following:

- **Required behaviour** — for example, what the situation demands. A dangerous task such as trampolining would require an autocratic rather than a democratic approach in order to maintain safety levels.
- **Actual behaviour** — for example, what style and approach the leader decides to take, and might be based on their own ability. The leader might considers all the factors and decide to adopt an autocratic style of leadership.
- **Preferred behaviour** — this is what style of leadership the performers would like best and is based on their own characteristics, such as ability. The group might like the autocratic approach because they find they develop their basic skills, and can therefore move onto more difficult skills quickly.

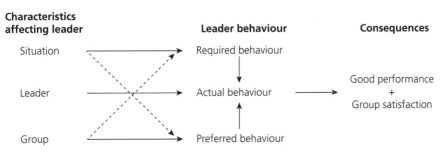

Figure 20 The Chelladurai model of leadership

Once these factors have been considered, the leader must try to balance their style of leadership with each of these in order to gain the highest level of performance and satisfaction from the group. The more the leader's actual behaviour matches what the group wants and what the situation needs, the better the performance will be. In the example given above, the leader decides to use the autocratic style. Because this matches what the group likes and what the situation needs, there is a greater chance that performance will improve and that the group will be satisfied.

Summary

After studying this topic you should be able to:
- give the characteristics of an effective leader
- describe the three styles of leadership and which situations each style is most effective with
- define and give examples of prescribed and emergent leaders
- explain Fiedler's and Chelladurai's model including sporting examples to illustrate

Stress management

Stress and stressors

Stress is how an individual responds to a threat. It is a negative response that causes anxiety, for example experiencing repetitive, negative thoughts in the weeks prior to a local derby.

Eustress is a positive response to a threat, for example feeling that you can overcome the challenge of completing a very difficult rock climb.

Stressors include:
- task importance, for example a final/local derby
- injury/fear of injury
- fear of failure
- social inhibition
- pressure from coach
- pressure to achieve extrinsic rewards, such as prize money
- high-level opponents

Exam tip

Students often find describing Chelladurai's model difficult. Keep the same example throughout and explain each part of the model whilst referring to it. Try working backwards through the model.

Eustress involves perceiving a situation as a positive challenge rather than as a threat.

Knowledge check 31

What is the difference between stress and eustress?

Cognitive effects of stress are psychological, for example negative/irrational thoughts.

Somatic effects of stress are physiological, for example increased heart rate and feeling nauseous.

Managing anxiety

Many performers experience high levels of anxiety. They should be taught a range of strategies that enable them to manage their anxiety levels (Table 15), including during training and warming up for competition.

Table 15 Strategies for managing anxiety levels

Cognitive strategies	Somatic strategies
Mental rehearsal — going over the performance in your mind, for example seeing all the subroutines of the triple jump without moving **Visualisation** — during training the image of the perfected skill is engrained into the memory and then relived during the performance **Imagery** — recalling a successful previous performance, using all the senses, including kinaesthesis, to recreate the feeling of success, for example remembering how the serve felt when you hit an ace **Thought stopping** — often used with above, for example a tennis player whose first serve is letting them down and begins to think 'I can't hit one in', should replace that thought with 'I can and I will hit the next one in' **Positive self-talk** — verbally reminding yourself of the key points of the movement, and telling yourself that you can achieve your goal, for example a rugby league player taking a conversion will talk himself through the run up, contact and follow through; he will tell himself that he can take the points, and might also have a mantra or saying that he continually repeats	**Biofeedback** — using equipment, such as a heart rate monitor reading bpm, while the performer undertakes the other various strategies described, generates physiological data showing which is the best method for them; these strategies are very effective but are time consuming, and using equipment during performance can distract athletes and increase anxiety levels because they are aware they are being monitored **Centring** — this is used alongside controlled breathing, and is useful during breaks in performance, i.e. time-outs or the end of a tennis set; the performer concentrates fully on their body (often the centre, i.e. the belly-button region) and breathes in; as they breathe out they chant a word or phrase relating to how they wish to perform (e.g. strong, focused, calm); this maintains focus on them, and any negative thoughts are disregarded **Breathing control** — by concentrating on and controlling the rate and depth of breathing the performer becomes less distracted, allowing them to focus on the task **Progressive muscular relaxation** — concentrate on each muscle group in turn; by tensing, holding then relaxing each group the performer begins to relax

Attentional control

Nideffer suggested that different activities require different types of attentional focus, for example invasion games require a broad focus, whereas net/wall games require a narrow style. Performers apply a variety of attentional styles, with the best athletes switching from one style to another.

There are two dimensions of focus:

- **Broad/narrow** — relating to how many cues are being focused on. Broad is many cues; narrow is one or two.
- **Internal/external** — relating to where the focus is being placed. Internal refers to the thoughts and feelings of the performers themselves; external focuses on the environmental cues.

Four attentional styles arise from this:

- **Broad-internal** — Focus on many cues concerning the performers themselves, for example a footballer planning their team strategies/next set piece.
- **Narrow-internal** — Focus on one or two cues concerning the performers themselves, and often used to calm nerves, for example a swimmer mentally rehearsing the sound of the starter signal and subsequent dive into the pool.
- **Broad-external** — Focus on many cues from the environment, for example a centre in netball focusing on many team-mates to whom she could pass.
- **Narrow-external** — Focus on one or two cues from the environment, for example a basketball player focusing on the net during a free throw.

During the performance the athlete concentrates on a range of environmental cues. If they can quickly distinguish what to focus on and selectively attend, i.e. pick out the correct cues, their performance will improve. They will not become distracted and can reduce the chance of information overload occurring. In addition, reaction time will improve. It also increases the likelihood of the performer entering the zone.

Cue utilisation

Easterbrook's **cue utilisation hypothesis** links a performer's ability to sustain focus on the correct cues in the environment with their level of arousal:

- At low levels of arousal the performer is not stimulated enough and takes in a large number of environmental cues. They are unable to distinguish what the relevant cues are and can become confused, reducing performance level.
- At high levels of arousal, the performer takes in a very small number of cues because they are excessively stimulated and may begin to panic. This is attentional wastage. The correct cues are missed, again reducing performance level.
- At moderate levels of arousal, the performer is able to selectively attend. They filter out the irrelevant cues and focus only on the relevant cues required. The performer completes the task to the highest level.

> **Exam tip**
>
> Ensure that you give a range of cognitive and somatic techniques when asked how to manage anxiety.

Summary

After studying this topic you should be able to:

- distinguish between stresses and stressors
- describe cognitive and somatic techniques and how they impact positively on the performer

Sport and society and the role of technology in physical activity and sport

Concepts of physical activity and sport

Physical recreation and sport

Sport and physical recreation have a number of different characteristics, including those identified in Table 16.

Table 16 Physical recreation compared with sport

	Physical recreation	Sport
Level of obligation	Available to all/choice	More selective
Rule structure	Rules can be modified, for example timings	Set rules apply, for example strict timings
Regulation	Self-officiated/self-regulated	External officials enforce rules
Motive	Mainly intrinsic rewards, participation focus and enjoyment as key motives	Extrinsic rewards available for success, for example winning medals; serious/competitive — end-result is important

The characteristics of physical education

The key characteristics of PE can be summarised as follows:

- It is compulsory.
- It involves formally taught lessons, with teachers in charge.
- It has four Key Stages as part of the National Curriculum, from ages 5–16.
- Lessons are pre-planned; it is highly structured.
- It is in school time.

Similarities and differences between physical recreation and PE

Physical recreation and PE are *similar* in that they both develop physical skills and are energetic, so have health and fitness benefits. They can both be fun to participate in, so have intrinsic benefits. The *differences* between physical recreation and physical education are summarised in Table 17.

Table 17 A comparison of physical recreation with physical education

Physical recreation	PE
Voluntary	Compulsory
In free time	In school time
Informal/relaxed	Formal teaching and learning
Self-regulated	Teacher in charge
Simple organisational structure	Highly structured

A comparison between the characteristics of PE and school sport

A direct comparison can be made between PE as a compulsory National Curriculum subject and school sport as a choice for young people (Table 18).

Table 18 National Curriculum PE compared with school sport

National Curriculum PE	School sport
In lesson time; curriculum time	In free time; extra-curricular
Compulsory	Element of choice; voluntary involvement
For all	For the chosen few; 'elitist'
Emphasis on taking part	Emphasis on winning
Teacher-led	Coaches involved
Wide variety of activities experienced	Specialisms develop

There are a number of common functions applicable to the different concepts of physical recreation, sport and PE, including the following, using the mnemonic 'POSITIVE' as a way of remembering them:

P Physical skills/competencies improve, increasing self-confidence.

O Occupies time in a positive way, i.e. social control.

S Social skills improve — friendships develop.

I Increased morality, for example in sharing/sportsmanship.

T Teamwork/leadership skills are developed.

I Increased health and fitness; development of healthy/active lifestyles.

V Variety of mental benefits, for example problem-solving/decision-making skills; stress relief).

E Enjoyment/fun/intrinsic benefits.

Summary

After studying this topic you should be able to:
- identify the characteristics and functions of key concepts (i.e. physical recreation, sport, physical education and school sport)
- understand the similarities and differences between these key concepts

Development of elite performers in sport

Factors required to support progression from talent ID to elite performance

Table 19 **Personal** and **sociocultural** factors required to support performer progression

Personal qualities	Sociocultural factors
Dedication/determination	Family support
Self-motivation/goal orientated	Equal opportunities/lack of discrimination
Self-confidence	Supportive family/educational provision
Natural talent/highly skilled	High levels of media coverage/access to role models/mentor support
High levels of physical fitness	Access to sports clubs/specialist coaches/training facilities

Personal qualities are the attributes and personality characteristics of an individual person, i.e. the physical and psychological attributes necessary for success in sport.

Sociocultural factors refer to the support required from wider society that is necessary for elite performer development.

The roles of organisations in developing elite performers

National governing bodies (NGBs)

NGBs of sport have a variety of roles/purposes in relation to elite performer development, including the following:

- Providing a specific focus on the development of the sport they are responsible for, for example elite performer development and winning medals in international sporting competitions. They liaise with other elite sport organisations, such as UK Sport.
- Promoting equality of opportunity for all to succeed in their sport.
- Developing effective talent ID schemes to maintain the 'talent factory' in their sport, for example the use of regional scouts.
- Allocating UK Sport World Class Performance Programmes (WCPP) funding/ Athlete Performance Awards in relation to their sport.
- Developing top-level coaches/a developmental coaching structure in their sport.
- Providing developmental training squads/progressive levels of competition to work through.
- Providing support services for elite performers via links with English Institute of Sport (EIS) centres, such as Performance Lifestyle advice.

National institutes of sport

National institutes of sport (e.g. the EIS) have the following roles:

- Offering a range of sport services to NGBs for developing elite performers, including sports science, biomechanics, psychology and technology.
- Providing Performance Lifestyle advice — a personalised support service for athletes on the WCPP, including time management and dealing with the media.
- Providing top-quality/world-class facilities, such as a high-performance environment to train in, medical and physio facilities, and the best coaches.
- Talent ID assessments, such as the UK Talent Team, operate a system to help deliver ongoing success by developing pathways for identifying and nurturing talent, for example talent recruitment and confirmation campaigns.
- Formerly known as Research and Innovation, the **Performance Innovation Team** looks at how technology and engineering can be used to develop kit/ equipment to give athletes an edge, for example marginal gains in winter 'sliding sports' via aerodynamic packages.

UK Sport

UK Sport's primary role is to invest National Lottery money into elite performer development, for example funding of their WCPP via NGBs. The WCPP covers all funded summer and winter Olympic and Paralympic sports. The two main levels of the WCPP are:

- **World Class Podium** — designed to support athletes with realistic medal-winning capabilities at the next Olympics/Paralympics (i.e. a maximum of 4 years away from the podium).

Knowledge check 34

Outline ways in which a national governing body can help ensure the development of elite performers.

The **Performance Innovation Team** based at the EIS enables accessibility to leading-edge technology and engineering for elite sports performers.

Knowledge check 35

The home nations of England, Northern Ireland, Scotland and Wales all have national institutes of sport. Describe how these national institutes are helping the development of the UK's elite athletes.

- **Podium Potential** — designed to support athletes whose performances suggest they have realistic medal-winning capabilities at subsequent Olympic/Paralympic Games (i.e. typically 4–6 years away from the podium).

Beneath Podium Potential is the **Talent level**, which provides funding and support to identify and confirm athletes who have the potential to progress to the pathway.

Other UK Sport roles include the following:

- Funding athletes directly to cover living/sporting costs via the **Athlete Performance Award** scheme.
- Overseeing and funding the EIS to ensure that resources are available to support Olympians/Paralympians, and to maximise their chances of medal success.
- Funding BOA Olympic and Paralympic preparation camps, for example Belo Horizonte for Rio 2016.
- Investing in events, for example the **Gold Event Series** (2013–23), which works closely with sports partners to ensure that the UK successfully bids for and stages the world's biggest sporting events. This can be via financial support for initial bids, or expertise/support with planning for, and delivery of, the actual event to help ensure its success, for example the World Athletics Championships in London 2017.
- Developing world-class coaches, for example via the UK Sport World Class Coaching Strategy, which aims to deliver innovative programmes to aid the development of world-class coaches, for example the Elite Coaching Apprenticeship Programme.
- It is the lead agency overseeing the running of **Talent ID** and **Performance Lifestyle** programmes.
- Developing and managing the UK's international sporting relationships, for example via the International Voice Programme.
- Operating **Mission 2016/18** to ensure 'continuous improvement' across Olympic and Paralympic funded sports.
- It has a cooperative/coordinated approach, working with other organisations involved in elite performer development, such as the EIS.

The **Gold Event Series** is UK Sport's major events programme for 2013–23.

Summary

After studying this topic you should be able to:

- identify the factors required to support progression from talent identification through to elite performance

- outline the roles of sports organisations in providing support and progression via schemes/initiatives to develop elite performance

---

Ethics in sport

There are seven sports ethics terms you need to be able to define and link to sporting examples, as identified in Table 20.

Table 20 Definitions of sports ethics terms

Ethics term	Definition
Amateurism	A nineteenth-century code of sporting ideals that involved participation in sport for the love of it, while receiving no monetary/financial gain
The Olympic Oath	A promise made by athletes/judges/coaches as representatives of their fellow competitors/officials/coaches to compete fairly and without doping — the maintenance of fair play
Sportsmanship	Conforming to the written and unwritten rules, and etiquette of sport, for example kicking the ball out of play when an opponent is injured
Gamesmanship	Stretching rules to the absolute limit without getting caught/punished, for example time wasting when winning
Win ethic	A 'win at all costs' approach to sport, for example drug taking
Positive deviance	Behaviour that is outside the norms of society, but with no intent to harm or break the rules, that involves over-adherence to the norms of society, for example competing when injured
Negative deviance	Behaviour that goes against the norms of society and has a detrimental effect on individuals and society in general, for example violence in sport

Exam tip

Sometimes sports ethics questions are set that require knowledge of the definitions and examples of more than one term. Answers must be clearly distinct, and state which sports ethics terms they are referring to; they also need to relate to correct examples to be awarded marks.

Summary

After studying this topic you should be able to:

- define a range of sports ethics terms, including amateurism, the Olympic Oath, sportsmanship, gamesmanship, win ethic, and positive and negative deviancy
- use suitable sporting examples to support these definitions

Knowledge check 36

Using practical examples, define what is meant by sportsmanship and gamesmanship?

Violence in sport

Causes of and strategies for preventing performer violence

The various causes of player violence can be remembered using the mnemonic 'WINNER':

W Win ethic and high rewards for success.

I Importance/emotional intensity of an event, such as a local derby

N Nature of the sport being aggressive, for example ice hockey

N National governing bodies are too lenient with their punishments.

E Excitement/over-arousal, for example caused by a coach team talk, or reaction to crowd abuse.

R Refereeing decisions are poor, leading to frustration.

Knowledge check 37

Outline possible reasons why an elite performer might act in an over-aggressive way that is deemed unacceptable by society.

A coach can use a range of strategies to reduce aggressive behaviour in a sports performer, such as:

- substituting them
- punishing aggressive behaviour, for example with fines
- increasing peer pressure, for example via the captain, to act less aggressively
- educating the performer/reinforcing use of assertive behaviour
- providing positive role model behaviour to aspire to
- highlighting their responsibility to the team/the negative impact on them if aggression leads to being sent off
- decreasing the emphasis on winning
- using stress management techniques, such as positive self-talk

NGBs can try to prevent player violence by:

- supporting the decisions of match officials when dealing with violence by performers, by using a **TMO** to check decisions being made, or changing/clarifying rules on violent acts such as high tackles
- punishing violence missed by officials after the match by using video evidence/ taking retrospective action as appropriate to the offence committed — fines and/or point deductions might be imposed on clubs for repeat offences of player violence
- using post-match video evidence, where individuals have been cited by referees as performing violent actions requiring further investigation, for example the rugby league 'on-report' system
- promoting performers with good disciplinary records as positive role models
- imposing punishments for violent actions on the field of play, for example sin bin/ booking
- introducing education campaigns/rewards linked to fair play, such as the FA's Respect campaign.

The **TMO** (television match official) is a referee who reviews TV footage of key events when asked to by the on-field referee.

Exam tip

Performer violence provides a possible synoptic link to sport psychology and theories of aggression.

Causes, control and implications of violence in sport

A variety of different factors can be identified as causing spectator violence, for example **football hooliganism**, including:

- emotional intensity and the ritual importance of the event, for example a local derby
- religious discord, for example Celtic vs Rangers
- too much alcohol and/or the 'highs' caused by drugs
- pre-match media hype stirring up tensions between rival fans
- poor policing, stewarding and crowd control, and lack of effective deterrents/ punishments to discourage individuals
- diminished responsibility for individuals in a large group, for example a football crowd; organised violence as part of a gang
- violence by players on the pitch reflected in the crowd
- violence sometimes used by young males as a display of their masculinity

Football hooliganism is violent behaviour by over-zealous supporters of association football clubs.

The strategies used to combat crowd violence at football matches include:

- banning/controlling alcohol sales
- improved use of police intelligence
- tougher deterrents, for example banning individuals from travelling abroad
- using CCTV to identify and then eject/arrest individuals for crowd disorder
- building all-seater stadiums and segregation of fans/family zones to create a more 'civilised' atmosphere
- encouraging responsible media reporting prior to matches
- playing games at kick-off times imposed by the police, for example early kick-offs to decrease alcohol consumption
- passing specific laws preventing 'trespass' onto the pitch, to try to stop pitch invasions/potential clashes between rival fans

Negative consequences of crowd violence for the sport of football include:

- a decline in participation rates
- lower spectator attendances
- supporters banned from attending matches
- all supporters being treated as hooligans
- teams being banned from competing/docked points/fined, which punishes the clubs for the acts of their supporters
- commercial deals being withdrawn due to the poor image of the game
- additional 'policing costs', lead to financial pressures on clubs at lower levels of the game
- declining relationships with other countries, leading to a negative impact on hosting future major competitions as a result of a poor reputation

Summary

After studying this topic you should be able to:

- identify and explain a variety of different causes and potential implications of violence in sport in relation to performers, spectators and sport
- outline strategies for helping to prevent violence occurring within sport, amongst performers as well as spectators

Drugs in sport

Social and psychological reasons for using illegal drugs and doping methods to aid performance

The **social reasons** for drug taking and using doping methods to enhance performance illegally include:

- a win-at-all-costs attitude
- the fame and fortune attached to success
- high levels of pressure to win, for example coaches/media expectations
- the lack of effective deterrents and a firm belief that they will not get caught
- poor role models setting a bad example, such as suggesting that drug taking in certain sports (e.g. cycling) is in some way acceptable

The **psychological reasons** for elite performers taking performance-enhancing drugs (PEDs) include:

■ steadying nerves — using beta blockers — in sports where fine motor control is required, for example snooker
■ increasing aggression — using anabolic steroids — in high-contact sports, such as rugby
■ raising self-belief — using stimulants — when athletes are suffering from a lack of confidence

The physiological effects of drugs

Table 21 The physiological effects of drugs on the performer and their performance

Method of enhancement	Description	Reasons why this method is used (i.e. physiological benefits)	Which athletes might use them?	Side-effects
Anabolic steroids	Artificially produced hormones, for example tetrahydrogestrinone (**THG**)	Aid in the storage of protein/promote muscle growth, leading to increased strength/power. Lead to less fat in the muscle; lean body weight. Can improve the body's capacity to train for longer at a higher intensity and decrease fatigue associated with training, enabling a faster recovery time	Power athletes, such as sprinters.	Liver damage. Heart and immune system problems. Acne and behaviour changes, such as aggression/mood swings
Betablockers	Help to calm an individual down/decrease anxiety by inhibiting the adrenaline that interferes with performance by preventing it from binding to nerve receptors	Improve accuracy in precision sports by steadying the nerves. Calm performance anxiety by keeping the heart rate low and decreasing any tremble in the hands. Widen the arteries, allowing increased blood flow and reducing involuntary muscle spasms	High-precision sports, such as archery and golf	Tiredness due to low blood pressure and slower heart rate, which will affect aerobic capacity
EPO	A natural hormone produced by the kidneys to increase red blood cells. Can now be artificially manufactured to cause an increase in haemoglobin levels	Stimulates red blood cell production, leading to an increase in the oxygen-carrying capacity of the body. This can result in an increase in the amount of work performed. It therefore increases endurance/delays the onset of fatigue — the athlete can keep going for longer/recover more quickly from training	Endurance performers such as long-distance cyclists	Can result in blood clotting, strokes and, possibly, death

---

Exam tip

The psychological/physiological effects (both positive and negative) of specified drugs are a new aspect of the 'social issues' section of the specification. Make sure you do not confuse *psychological* with *physiological*.

Knowledge check 39

Describe the physiological reasons why an elite performer might use anabolic steroids just like any other training aid.

The negative implications for the sport and the performer of drug taking

Drug taking threatens the integrity of **sport**. It is cheating, and negatively damages the reputation of a sport, reducing interest in it.

For the **performer** it provides negative role models, who set a bad example for youngsters. It can also be very damaging to a performer's health. There are a number of negative social consequences:

- Athletes involved in doping may lose their good reputation following a positive test.
- Future career prospects may be negatively impacted, with a loss of income/sponsorship deals resulting from doping infringements being widely reported in the media.
- It can result in legal action against individuals, who could be banned from competing, and stripped of medals and earnings.

Strategies for the elimination of PEDs in sport

A range of strategies can be used in the battle to eliminate PEDs in sport. You can remember drug elimination strategies using the mnemonic 'DOPING':

D Drug-free culture created via education programmes, for example 100% Me, using positive role models.

O Organisations involved in drug detection/enforcement work together, for example UKAD/NGBs.

P Punishments need to be harsher to act as effective deterrents.

I Investment into new technology/random testing, for example the **whereabouts system**.

N Name and shame negative role models.

G Guilty lose (Lottery) funding/sponsorship deals.

Arguments for and against drug taking and testing

Various arguments can be used *for* the legalisation of drugs in sport:

- The battle against drugs is expensive/time consuming.
- Drugs are quite easily accessible/very difficult to eliminate.
- Detection is not always effective because new drugs become available/masking agents are developed.
- Sometimes it is difficult to define what is a 'drug', compared with a legal supplement.
- Drugs are sometimes taken accidentally.
- Sacrifices made by a performer are personal choice; if everyone takes drugs, it levels the playing field and increases performance standards.
- If drug taking is properly monitored, health risks may be lessened.
- Athletes do not ask to be role models and individuals have a right to choose because it is their body.

Most people, however, would argue *against* the points above and point out that drugs should continue to be banned in sport for the following reasons:

- There are health risks/dangerous side-effects, for example heart disorders.
- The creation of negative role models sets a poor example to youngsters.

The **whereabouts system** is an out-of-competition testing system that requires athletes to provide details of their location, so they can be accessed at any time and anywhere for testing.

- Drugs create a negative image for certain sports, for example weight lifting and cycling.
- There is increasing pressure to take drugs, for example from coaches and peers who take drugs.
- Success in sport should be about hard work and natural talent — drug use is outside this concept.
- Drugs give an unfair advantage/are unethical — their use is cheating/illegal.

Summary

After studying this topic you should be able to:
- explain the social and psychological reasons why elite performers use illegal PEDs
- explain the physiological impact of EPO, anabolic steroids and beta blockers on sports performance
- discuss the implications of drug taking for sport and sports performers
- outline strategies used to try to eliminate the use of PEDs in sport
- discuss the arguments for and against drug taking and testing

Sport and the law

The uses of sports legislation

Performers

Sports performers face many potential issues that require legal services, including the following:

- **Contractual disputes** with their clubs (i.e. employers) — many of these relate to 'freedom of contract' for footballers, resulting from the **Bosman ruling**.
- Contractual disputes with their sponsors — these include breach of contract issues, for example via negative actions such as doping/violent conduct, which impact negatively on the sponsor's image.
- **Injury/loss of earnings** (i.e. damages) — some sports performers have sought legal redress/compensation for the 'deliberate/harmful actions' of an opponent (e.g. a dangerous tackle); loss of earnings claims can also result from inequality issues (e.g. the sex discrimination case of the USA women's soccer team vs their soccer federation), as well as false doping bans (e.g. Diane Modahl vs British Athletics Federation).

Officials

Negligence is when someone, for example an official, fails to take 'reasonable care' over another person to avoid any dangers that could cause them harm. Officials have a **duty of care** towards participants to make sure that all dangers around them are eliminated, so they can participate in a safe environment. When the officials do not do 'everything possible' to keep participants safe, they might be viewed as being 'negligent' — for example, allowing a match to be played on a dangerous surface that has not been checked prior to kick-off.

The **Bosman ruling** is a ruling by the European Court of Justice that gave a professional football player within the EU the right to a free transfer at the end of their contract.

Knowledge check 40

Outline the reasons why sports performers might need protection from the law during their sporting careers.

Coaches

The duty of care means that sports coaches have a legal obligation to eliminate all potential dangers so that players can participate in a safe environment, and to ensure that nobody gets hurt 'unnecessarily'. In the sporting environment, especially when working with young people, coaches should ensure that they follow a number of steps to demonstrate a duty of care:

- Risk assessment (RA) — ensuring that they have carried out an appropriate risk assessment for the activities being coached, so that any dangers can be planned for.
- First aid (FA) — ensuring that first aid provision is available at the venue where the coaching is taking place.
- Supervision ratios for the activity (SA) — maintaining appropriate supervision ratios depending on the activity being coached, age/experience of group being coached etc.
- Data to access/contact details (DA) — keeping up-to-date attendance records, contact details and medical details so that information can be used/contact can be made in an emergency.

> **Exam tip**
>
> You can remember the ways in which a coach can ensure a duty of care using the mnemonic RAFA SADA.

Spectators

A variety of different measures have been introduced to try to ensure crowd safety/ overcome hooliganism at football matches:

- Ground safety — removal of perimeter fences and all-seater stadia to replace the terraces. A fire security certificate is required from the local authority for an event to happen.
- Alcohol controls — control of alcohol sales on the way to grounds/within them.
- Police/security measures — specified kick-off times imposed by police.
- Increased security and police presence — intelligence gathering and improved police liaison between forces across the country/the world.
- Tougher deterrents, such as banning orders — supporters face legal consequences for behaviour such as running onto the pitch, i.e. trespass, and assaulting players.

> **Exam tip**
>
> The use of sports legislation to control hooliganism is a potential synoptic question linking to strategies for preventing violence within sport in relation to the spectator.

> **Summary**
>
> After studying this topic you should be able to explain the various uses of sports legislation in relation to the performer, official, coach and spectator.

Impact of commercialisation and the relationship between sport and the media

The positive and negative impacts of commercialisation, sponsorship and the media

Tables 21–25 outline how increasing media coverage and the **commercialisation of sport** have impacted in positive and negative ways.

Commercialisation of sport links modern-day sport to business/commerce.

Performers

Table 22 Positive and negative impacts of sponsorship and commercial deals on elite sports performers

Positives	Negatives
Increased wages, prize money	A win-at-all-costs attitude to maintain high-level prize money, wages, sponsorship deals etc.
Increased availability of professional contracts, where performers are able to devote themselves full time to sport to improve performance	An increase in 'deviant' behaviour due to increased pressure to win, for example performing when injured or over-training
Performers are increasingly in the public eye, so they need to behave appropriately to protect a positive image	Sponsors become too demanding, for example expecting personal appearances at sponsorship events when the performer should be training
Increased funding to pay for access to high-quality training support etc.	Inequality of funding means that performers in minority sports, such as badminton, miss out on funding/full-time professional opportunities

Coaches

Table 23 Positive and negative impacts of increased media coverage and commercialisation of elite sport on coaches/managers

Minority sports are those with low levels of interest/participation.

Positives	Negatives
Gain an increased profile, raising public awareness of their role	Increased pressure to be successful and win matches
Increased salaries on offer, for example in football	The expectation to deal with the media (which is often linked to contracts such as that between the Premier League and Sky) and answer their questions can be particularly difficult
Increased funding from sponsors/sale of media rights, which is then invested into the sport, enables investment into improving playing squads and support systems, such as training grounds and medical provision	Inequalities of funding mean that coaches/managers in lower-level clubs/minority sports find it harder to attract the best performers to their clubs/sports, which means they are financially disadvantaged

Officials

Table 24 Positive and negative impacts of commercialisation of elite sport on officials/referees

Positives	Negatives
Increased profile raising public awareness of their important role in ensuring fairness in sport	Risk of possible demotion/job loss if a faulty decision is highlighted in the media
Increased wages/sponsorships and possibility of full-time employment as part of an elite group of match officials, for example Premier League football	High rewards at stake — may lead to bribery/increased pressure on officials to get decisions right
Increased funding to invest in technology/support systems and training to improve standards of officiating	Technology to aid officials in their decision making is not always available to them at 'lower levels' of a sport
	Over dependence on media technology when it is made available to officials may lead to decreased confidence to make their own decisions

Spectators/the audience

Table 25 Positive and negative impact of increased media coverage and commercialisation of elite sport for spectators/the audience

Positives	Negatives
Increased performance standards provide a high level of entertainment	Increased cost of watching sport, for example via pay-per-view channels
Improved quality of facilities resulting from increased investment	Fewer tickets available for the fans, with more allocated to sponsors/corporate hospitality
Improved viewing experience via media innovations, such as interactive technology, and increased opportunities to watch live events	Links to team or player merchandise are sometimes viewed negatively due to the high cost/regularity of change
Availability of **merchandise** encourages team loyalty, for example via the purchase and subsequent wearing of a team's kit	Minority sports receive less coverage
Variations in a sport's format develop, providing alternative viewing experiences, such as 20/20 cricket	Increased number of breaks in play to accommodate adverts/decisions of officials
Increased excitement in the audience whilst awaiting the decisions of off-field officials, for example Hawkeye in tennis	Changes in kick-off times to maximise viewing figures (i.e. scheduled at prime time), which is not always in the best interests of fans travelling long distances
Increased awareness and knowledge of sport; creation of role models for fans to idolise	Loss of the traditional nature of the sport, for example cricket whites being replaced by coloured kit
Increased elimination of negative aspects of sport, such as player violence	

Merchandise refers to goods that promote the team and associated sponsors.

Knowledge check 41

Explain the benefits to the audience of increased media coverage of sport.

Sport

Table 26 Positive and negative effects of commercialisation and sponsorship on sport

Positive effects	Negative effects
Increased funding provides improved facilities, equipment and coaching to help develop performers in that sport	Sports might become over-reliant on the funding and experience problems if it is withdrawn
Increased funding provides technology at events to aid decision making among officials	Inequalities of funding mean that football is highly attractive to sponsors, while a sport like hockey is not
Increased spectator interest and involvement, for example by wearing the team kit	Traditionalists might be against new competitions, coloured clothing, or changes in a sport's format
Increased number of events and competitions helps generate interest/promote a sport	The location of events may be influenced by commercial considerations, for example American Football at Wembley to help the global appeal of the game

Summary

After studying this topic you should be able to discuss the positive and negative impacts of commercialisation, sponsorship and the media on performers, coaches, officials, spectators/the audience and sport.

The role of technology in physical activity and sport

Understanding of technology for sports analytics

Video and analysis programmes

Coaches and athletes are using digital technology as a medium more and more to analyse individual techniques, as well as team performances. At an individual level, video analysis can be used to analyse gait and biomechanical aspects of performance, with any information gained also being potentially helpful in rehabilitation from injury.

Video motion analysis usually involves a high-speed camera and computer with software (e.g. Dartfish), allowing frame-by-frame playback of the footage. It is useful in individual analysis of technical performance, for example to identify and correct problems with an athlete's technique, such as the angle of release when throwing a discus.

Testing and recording equipment (metabolic cart for indirect calorimetry)

A **metabolic cart** is an electronic medical tool for measuring the body's metabolism through the amount of heat produced when the body is at rest, using a process called calorimetry. The result can inform medics more about a person's overall health condition. The various parts of the device, which include a computer system, monitor and breathing tubes, are typically mounted together on a mobile push-cart, hence the name, so that it can easily be moved from one room to another.

Indirect calorimetry involves attaching the headgear from the cart to a subject while they breathe for a specific length of time. The subject's inspired and expired gas flows, volumes and concentrations of oxygen and carbon dioxide are all continually measured. These measurements are then translated into a heat equivalent. It is a non-invasive technique and is regarded as relatively accurate.

Indirect calorimetry and use of a metabolic cart can help individuals:

- determine their energy requirements/response to nutrition over time
- calculate energy expenditure, allowing determination of nutritional requirements/calorific needs
- who are classified/potentially classified as obese

Use of GPS technology and motion-tracking software and hardware

GPS (global positioning system) technology gives a vast amount of information immediately. It is used to:

- track the speed achieved, distance run, directions taken and dynamic acceleration of the individual concerned, while measuring heart rate and recovery time
- provide precise/valid data for helping performance by monitoring success rates in various aspects of technical performance, for example number of successful passes
- measure impact in G forces in high-contact sports, such as rugby, to help improve player safety
- help coaches to make objective decisions about possible substitutions, for example by monitoring a performer's fatigue level, thus helping to decrease injury risk
- manage workload during rehabilitation

When discussing/evaluating the use of GPS technology in sport, it is important to consider possible negative implications of using such technology, including the following:

- Pure data can be misleading at times, for example if a performer has not covered many metres in a game, but the tactics and game context are such that it does not require them to do so. They can also sometimes be 'unreliable' if the GPS is not used correctly or is misinterpreted by coaches.
- It can be expensive, so inequalities might exist in terms of access to the latest technology.

Video motion analysis is used to extract information about moving objects from video.

A **metabolic cart** is a device for measuring the body's metabolism by calculating the amount of heat produced.

Knowledge check 42

Define the terms indirect calorimetry and metabolic cart.

GPS is a space-based navigation system that provides location and time information, which is increasingly being used by professional sports teams.

- Players and coaches might become too reliant on data to inform their decision making, and be unable to react creatively and instantly to on-field problems as they occur.
- Athletes might gain increased confidence by using the equipment, even though there may be limited scientific proof to support its effectiveness.
- While GPS and the data it provides are usually relatively accurate/reliable, with the ability to provide useful real-time data, there are situations when such reliability can be negatively affected, for example by poorly maintained equipment/errors occurring when coaches do not know how to use it correctly.

Functions of sports analytics

Use of technology in injury prevention

Possible health benefits from **vibration therapy** include:

- improved bone density, muscle power and circulation
- an overall reduction in joint pain/delayed onset of muscle soreness
- alleviation of stress
- a boost to metabolism
- maintenance of cartilage integrity where weight-bearing activities are difficult to undertake

Electrostimulation can aid injury prevention by:

- strengthening muscles
- helping to prevent losses in fitness levels via application to specific muscle groups, to maintain muscle tone during periods of inactivity
- assisting in rehabilitation through the gradual strengthening of injured or weakened muscles
- helping to get rid of lactic acid after a training session or competition
- decreasing muscle tension/potential injury by providing a relaxing effect on the muscles

Vibration therapy, also known as 'whole body vibration' (WBV), involves the use of vibration plates to induce exercise effects in the body.

Electrostimulation is the production of muscle contraction using electrical impulses.

The development of equipment and facilities in sport

Impact of material technology on adapted equipment for the elderly and disabled

Highly advanced equipment has been developed for elite Paralympians, while devices are also being created to help elderly and disabled sports enthusiasts participate at a recreational level. In athletics, different designs of adaptive equipment, such as specially designed wheelchairs, are used on the track, while in the field, throwing frames have been developed for use in the shotput and discus.

Wheelchairs can be individually designed and adapted to meet the specific requirements of different sports. For example, tennis requires lightweight frames to enable fast-paced movements, while contact sports (e.g. rugby) require chairs with strong frames and impact/foot protection.

Prosthetic devices have been specially developed for a number of athletic applications. For example, prosthetic leg designs offer improved gait efficiency to assist athletes in running.

Facilities—Olympic legacy, surfaces, multi-use

Places People Play is an initiative introduced by Sport England that aims to deliver on the Olympic legacy promise to increase sports participation by providing sports facilities for the local community to use. Iconic Facilities is part of this initiative, designed to transform the places people use to play sport across the country. The Iconic Facilities fund directs money into a small number of 'best practice' facility projects designed to increase mass participation in sport across England. Best practice is based on high-quality design and long-term sustainability of a facility, to deliver multi-sport provision with a focus on sporting activities that have high participant numbers.

There have been a number of technological developments in creating surfaces that are suitable for such multi-sport provision, with **3G surfaces** increasingly being used. 3G artificial grass is a sand and rubber infilled synthetic surface, which is ideal for sports such as hockey and football. It can be played on more frequently than natural grass and therefore allows high levels of use for a wide variety of sports. Synthetic grass also gives consistent conditions, which can aid the technical development of performers, whereas natural grass can become very worn and unpredictable.

One of the main problems for sports such as football is that some synthetic surfaces do not truly reflect the bounce of grass. In addition, they have been criticised for being too rigid, leading to more joint/ligament injuries.

3G surfaces are third-generation synthetic grass pitches suitable for multi-sport provision.

The role of technology in sport and its positive and negative impacts

There are a number of potential advantages and disadvantages of technology for sports performers (Table 27).

Table 27 Positives and negatives of technology for sports performers

Positives	Negatives
Improved clothing/footwear/equipment can lead to better performances, for example bodysuits used by sprinters to increase speed	Technology could encourage passive consumers, for example via watching sport
Improved protective equipment, for example cricket helmets to withstand fast bowling	Use of labour-saving devices, such as Segways, as a replacement for walking can decrease physical activity levels
Improved recovery from training/injury, for example compression clothing to help improve circulation	It can lead to injury/over-aggression, for example protective equipment can make some performers feel less inhibited
Detailed scientific analysis of performance, for example via GPS data, to provide meaningful technical and physiological feedback to performers/coaches	It can be expensive and unaffordable for some, leading to potential inequalities/unfair advantages if the technology is not available to all
	The availability of technological advancements for aiding performance might be dependent on an individual or team sponsor, which might positively or negatively influence the chances of success
Increased knowledge of diet and sports supplements, for example carbo-loading	It can lead to increased use of illegal performance-enhancing drugs, for example through the development of effective masking agents or new PEDs for which there are no tests
Advancements in drug-testing technology to keep up with performers taking illegal performance-enhancing drugs	It can cause long delays/disruption in sport, which can impact negatively on the performer, for example having to await the review decision of an official
Improved confidence in officiating, for example using a TMO	

Exam tip

Make sure that you can evaluate the impacts of technology on sports, performers, coaches and the audience.

Sporting audiences have benefited from advancements in technology through:

- increased sense of crowd excitement/involvement, for example awaiting decisions via a big screen (e.g. Hawk-Eye)
- improved experience of watching sport at home, for example HD/split-screen coverage
- increased excitement from watching higher-level performances resulting from technological advancements
- a wider range of sports being accessible as a result of media advancements/satellite technology

Summary

After studying this topic you should be able to:

- understand key terms used in sports analytics
- explain the use of different methods of collecting sports analytics data and the functions such information can fulfil

- explain the impact of facility/equipment development on participation and performance
- discuss the positives and negatives of technology linked to sports, performers, coaches and the audience

Knowledge check 43

How have sports spectators benefited from advancements in technology?

Questions & Answers

This section explains the structure of AQA A-level Physical Education Paper 2 (7582) and discusses strategies for approaching the different types of questions you will encounter. This is followed by a series of sample questions covering all the question types — multiple choice, short answer and extended writing. Each question is followed by a sample student answer, with accompanying comments. You should practise all of these questions yourself and compare your answers with these, while reading the comments on the answers to improve your understanding of what is required to achieve full marks.

Exam format

Paper 2 of your PE A-level is divided into three sections to match the specification. In the exam each section is worth 35 marks and starts with a multiple-choice question. There are 12 marks available for short-answer questions (including multiple choice), and then there are two extended questions worth 8 marks and 15 marks. You have 2 hours to try to earn the 105 marks available. This paper counts for 35% of your A-level.

The extended-answer questions are marked using a levels-based scheme; some short-answer questions worth 6 marks can also be marked in this way. Your examiner will not just count up the number of AO1 marks (knowledge), AO2 marks (application/examples) and AO3 marks (analysis/evaluation). They will use a marking grid, which can be found on the AQA website, and highlight your answers using the following categories to come to an overall judgement:

- AO1 — knowledge
- AO2 — application
- AO3 — analysis/evaluation
- relevant terminology
- reasoning, clarity, structure and focus

(In the sample answers to extended and 6-mark questions in this section, each assessment objective has been labelled (AO1, AO2 and AO3), so it is easier for you to see where the answer demonstrates knowledge, application and analysis/evaluation.)

For the 15-mark questions there are 4 marks available for AO1, 5 marks for AO2 and 6 marks for AO3. If no AO3 is evident at all in your answer, then a maximum of 9 marks only can be awarded.

For the 8-mark questions there are 2 marks available for AO1, 3 marks for AO2 and 3 marks for AO3. If no AO3 is evident at all in your answer, then a maximum of 5 marks only can be awarded.

Across Paper 1 and Paper 2 there will be two 15-mark questions and one 8-mark question that will be 'synoptic'. This means that the question could ask for any of the following:

- Knowledge, application and analysis/evaluation of two topics from the same section, for example:
  - Exercise physiology and biomechanics — diet and training
  - Sport psychology — arousal and aggression
  - Sport and society and the role of technology in sport — ethics and drugs
- Knowledge, application and analysis/evaluation of two topics from different sections, for example:
  - Exercise physiology and biomechanics/Sports psychology
  - Sport and society and the role of technology in sport/Sport psychology
  - Sport and society/Exercise physiology and biomechanics
- Knowledge, application and analysis/evaluation of one topic from any section in Paper 1 with another topic from any section in Paper 2.

If there is more than one topic in the question, try to link the topics where possible. If you do not do this, you will not be able to access the top level.

Finally, in the exam it is important that you write clearly in the spaces provided in the answer booklet. Avoid writing anything that you want to be marked in the margins, and always indicate if you run out of space that your answer continues on additional paper.

Exam comments

Each question is followed by a brief analysis of what to watch out for when answering the question. All student responses are then followed by examiner's comments. In the weaker answers, they also point out areas for improvement, specific problems and common errors, such as lack of clarity, weak or non-existent development, irrelevance, misinterpretation of the question and mistaken meanings of terms.

■ Exercise physiology and biomechanics

Diet and nutrition and their effect on physical activity and performance

Question 1

Evaluate how using the supplement creatine can improve a sprinter's performance.   [6 marks]

> The key word here is *evaluate*. Some 6-mark questions can be assessed using banded marking. You need to make sure you go through all the assessment objectives (AO1, AO2 and AO3), so give knowledge of creatine, apply your knowledge and then evaluate/justify why it might be used.

Student A answer

Creatine is a supplement that can be used by power athletes, who use the ATP-PC system, because it helps this system to last longer AO1 and improves recovery times AO1. However, the side-effects of taking creatine include cramping, bloating and nausea AO1. A 100 m sprinter benefits the most from taking creatine, as opposed to a 400 m sprinter, because the 100 m lasts approximately 10 seconds for elite performers, and so they use the ATP-PC system AO2. Creatine increases the strength and power of the 100 m sprinter because it also increases muscle mass AO2.

Creatine is also a legal supplement, so it is fair for a 100 m sprinter to use it, and means there is no cheating. AO3 However, it is important for the sprinter to consider the side-effects because cramping, bloating and nausea could have a detrimental effect on performance AO3 and, in addition, some research indicates that the effect of creatine on performance is inconclusive AO3.

6/6 marks awarded Student A has correctly gone through each of the assessment objectives, showing their knowledge of creatine and applying it well to a 100 m sprinter. They have also evaluated the use of creatine in relation to the sprinter.

Student B answer

Creatine is a supplement that can be used to increase performance by increasing muscle mass AO1. Taking creatine helps to replenish the PC stores, to allow the ATP-PC system to last for longer and recover more quickly AO1. Many athletes take creatine because it is a legal way of increasing the size and strength of their muscles AO1, but the side-effects of taking creatine include cramping, bloating and nausea AO1.

2/6 marks awarded Student B has only demonstrated knowledge of creatine. There is no application, evaluation or justification with regards to a sprinter. Always make sure that you refer to any example given in a question in your answer.

Preparation and training methods in relation to maintaining physical activity and performance

Question 2

Evaluate the appropriateness of continuous training and interval training for a 100m sprinter and for a 10000m runner.

[8 marks]

> This is an extended 8-mark question, so the marking grid will be used to assess the answer. You need to make sure you give your knowledge of both continuous training and interval training, applying them to both the 100m and the 10000m, and then evaluate the appropriateness of each type of training for these performers. AO1 2 marks; AO2 3 marks; AO3 3 marks

Student A answer

Interval training is used to improve anaerobic power AO1. It is a form of training in which periods (intervals) of high-intensity work are followed by active recovery periods AO1. Continuous training develops aerobic endurance AO1 and involves low-intensity exercise for long periods of time, for example jogging AO1.

The 100m runner needs anaerobic power to win their event, so interval training is suitable because it increases speed AO2. The 10000m runner will concentrate more on continuous training because they need to develop aerobic endurance and work for long periods of time at a lower intensity AO2. In interval training the duration of the work intervals can be changed and adapted to work on weaknesses. If the start of the race needs improvement, then the 100m sprinter could choose shorter work intervals, such as 30m or 40m AO2.

Continuous training is not appropriate for the 100m sprinter due to its aerobic nature AO3. Interval training is appropriate because the sprinter needs to concentrate on extending the use of the ATP/PC system, so that they do not rely on the slower anaerobic glycolytic system at the end of the race AO3. Therefore, they will choose work intervals of up to 10 seconds AO2. However, they should not just rely on interval training because there are other methods of training that are also appropriate. Weight training, for example, is necessary to develop strength and power, which the sprinter needs to run fast AO3.

7/8 marks awarded Student A addresses all AO1, AO2 and AO3 areas. The knowledge (AO1) of both training methods is excellent, and application (AO2) to the 100m and 10000m is consistently made. However, this level 3 answer fails to score the maximum mark because there is no evaluation of the appropriateness of these training methods for a 10000m runner. Students regularly fail to address part of a question. Always check through your response to a question, and for the extended questions make sure you plan carefully at the start to avoid this.

Otherwise the answer has the required breadth and depth, with relevant terminology throughout, and is written clearly with relevant focus.

Student B answer

Interval training is where there are work intervals of high-intensity work followed by active recovery periods AO1. Continuous training involves low-intensity exercise for long periods of time AO1. A 100m runner will use interval training to improve their speed because it is suitable for this AO2. A 10000m runner will use continuous training to develop their endurance, which is appropriate for the 10000m as it is an endurance event AO2.

3/8 marks awarded This answer is too brief and does not have enough depth. There is evidence of knowledge of each type of training, but application to the 100m and 10000m is limited. There is no evaluation of the appropriateness of each type of training for each event, so there are no AO3 marks awarded. The answer is therefore awarded a mark from the bottom of level 2.

Injury prevention and the rehabilitation of injury

Question 3

Identify which **one** of the following statements is correct.

[1 mark]

A Achilles tendonitis is an acute injury

B A muscle strain is a chronic injury

C Tennis elbow is a chronic injury

D A dislocation is a chronic injury

There will be multiple-choice questions in your exam. Make sure you follow the instructions on how to answer them very carefully.

Student A answer

C Tennis elbow is a chronic injury.

1/1 mark awarded This answer is correct. An acute injury occurs when pain is felt immediately, while a chronic injury is an over-use injury. These terms can be easily confused.

Student B answer

C Tennis elbow is a chronic injury.

0/1 mark awarded Although Student A has identified the correct answer, they have not followed the instructions. On your exam paper you have to fill in the circle because the multiple-choice answers are scanned and not marked by examiners.

Biomechanical principles

Question 4

As a rugby player prepares to tackle, identify and explain the factors he needs to consider to increase his stability.

[3 marks]

Here you need to identify the four factors that affect stability that are on the specification, relate them to the rugby player and then explain how he uses them as he prepares to tackle.

Student A answer

As the rugby player prepares for a tackle, he needs to make sure he lowers his centre of mass to make him more stable on contact. ✓ He also needs to widen his support base by keeping his feet wide apart. ✓ His line of gravity needs to be central over his feet. ✓ Also the more weight the rugby player has the more stable he will become. ✓

3/3 marks awarded Student A has written more scoring points than required. The factors that affect stability are correctly identified and explained in relation to the rugby player preparing to tackle.

Student B answer

A rugby player needs to consider the following factors: the height of his centre of mass, the area of his support base, the position of his line of gravity and his body mass.

0/3 marks awarded This answer correctly identifies the factors that affect stability, but scores no marks because there is no explanation of these factors in relation to the rugby player preparing to tackle an opponent. Always look at the command terms in the question. In this case they are *identify* and *explain*.

Levers

Question 5

Name and sketch the lever system that operates during plantar flexion of the ankle. [3 marks]

In this question you need to decide which class of lever system plantar flexion of the ankle is — first, second or third. After naming the lever system you need to sketch it, adding fulcrum, resistance and effort in the correct order.

Student A answer

Plantar flexion is a second-order lever. ✓

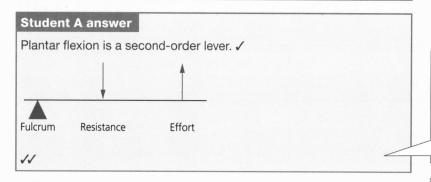

Fulcrum   Resistance   Effort

✓✓

3/3 marks awarded Plantar flexion of the ankle is correctly identified as a second-order lever. The sketch is drawn accurately, with all three labels and resistance in the middle. It does not matter which way round the fulcrum and the effort are.

Student B answer

Plantar flexion is a second-order lever. ✓

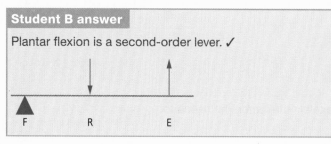

F   R   E

1/3 marks awarded Student B correctly identifies plantar flexion as a second-class lever. However, although the sketch is correct, the use of abbreviations is not creditworthy. The exam board will accept some abbreviations for terms, but make sure you know which these are. If you are unsure, then do not abbreviate.

Linear motion

Question 6

Identify and explain two forces acting on a triple jumper at take-off. [4 marks]

Here you need to identify the forces, such as weight (gravity) and air resistance, and explain the effect that each of these has on the triple jumper.

Student A answer

The first force acting on a triple jumper is weight ✓, which acts in a downward direction pushing the performer back towards the track and the sand pit ✓. Another force is air resistance ✓, which acts in a horizontal direction, opposing motion ✓.

4/4 marks awarded Student A correctly identifies two forces and then goes on to explain the effect they have on the triple jumper. They could also have chosen friction, which occurs when the triple jumper's spikes make contact with the track, allowing them to move forwards.

Student B answer

Two forces acting on the triple jumper are weight ✓ and friction ✓.

2/4 marks awarded Student B has only addressed one part of the question, failing to explain the forces. Always read the question carefully and highlight the command terms to ensure that your answer covers all aspects of the question.

Angular motion

Question 7

Explain how a 10 m diver can alter her speed of rotation by changing her body shape. [5 marks]

This question wants you to write about the conservation of angular momentum. Any question on this topic has three key terms you need to address: angular momentum, angular velocity and moment of inertia.

Student A answer

When the diver rotates, her angular momentum remains constant. ✓ Angular momentum = moment of inertia × angular velocity. ✓ Angular momentum refers to the quantity of her rotation. ✓ Moment of inertia is how the diver distributes her mass around her axis of rotation ✓, and angular velocity refers to the speed of the rotation during the dive ✓. If the diver changes her moment of inertia, it leads to a change in the angular velocity of her rotation. ✓ For example, if she takes her arms and legs further away from her axis of rotation and starts to open up her body in preparation for entry into the water, this will allow her to decrease the speed of her rotation. ✓

5/5 marks awarded This answer explains fully the relationship between angular momentum, moment of inertia and angular velocity. There is excellent application of these in relation to changing body shape, and the effect this has on the speed of rotation.

Student B answer

The diver can alter her speed of rotation by changing her body shape. If she wants to spin faster she brings her arms and legs in, and if she wants slow her spin down she moves her arms and legs out. ✓

1/5 marks awarded Student B has correctly identified how changing body shape affects the speed of rotation. However, there is only an example and no explanation of the theory behind this. Answers on the mechanics of spin need to mention angular momentum, angular velocity and moment of inertia, and the relationship between them.

Projectile motion

Question 8

In a game of badminton, a player will hit the shuttlecock into the air to cross the net, and it then becomes a projectile. Explain how the various forces act to affect the shuttlecock during its flight.

[3 marks]

> You need to identify the forces as weight (or gravity) and air resistance, and explain the effect that each of these has on the flight path of the shuttlecock. When weight is the larger of the two forces, the projectile follows a parabolic flight path. If air resistance is the larger of the two forces, a non-parabolic flight path is the result.

Student A answer

Two external forces act on the shuttlecock. Weight or gravity reduces height as it pushes the shuttlecock downwards, acting on the vertical component. ✓ Air resistance opposes motion ✓, and this will have a big effect on the shuttlecock because it is very light and has an irregular shape ✓. When air resistance is the bigger of the two forces, which is the case with a shuttlecock, it will follow a non-parabolic flight path. ✓

3/3 marks awarded Student A has correctly identified weight/gravity and air resistance as the two forces that act on a projectile. They have then applied this knowledge by explaining the effect these two forces have on the shuttlecock, and the flight path the shuttlecock consequently takes.

Student B answer

Gravity pushes the shuttlecock towards the ground ✓ and air resistance opposes motion ✓.

2/3 marks awarded The forces are correctly identified, but more application to the shuttlecock and its flight path is needed for full marks.

Fluid mechanics

Question 9

Explain the Bernoulli principle in relation to an upward lift force for a discus thrower.

[4 marks]

> To answer this question you need to explain air flow above and below the discus, and identify how this creates an upward lift force on the discus.

Student A

An upward lift force during flight means that the discus can stay in the air for longer, which increases the horizontal distance it travels. ✓ In terms of the Bernoulli principle, the air that travels over the top of the discus has to travel a longer distance than the air underneath. ✓ This means the air above the discus travels faster, which therefore creates a lower pressure. ✓ The air that travels under the discus has to travel a shorter distance than the air above. This means the air below the discus travels slower, which therefore creates a higher pressure. ✓ The higher pressure below the discus then creates an upward lift force and allows the discus to travel further. When the discus is released, the angle of attack is important. ✓ The optimum angle of attack is anything between 25° and 40°. ✓

4/4 marks awarded Bernoulli's principle is described correctly and applied to the discus throw. In addition, Student A explains the importance of the angle of attack and gives an example.

Student B answer

The discus has an upward lift force because the air that travels over the top of the discus travels a shorter distance than the air underneath. As a result, the air above the discus travels at a slower velocity and a higher pressure. This creates an upward lift force.

0/4 marks awarded Student has described how a *downward* lift force is created. This is a simple mistake to make. High pressure needs to be underneath the discus if it is to create an upward lift force.

Biomechanical principles and projectile motion

Question 10

Explain Newton's first and second laws of motion in relation to the shot put, and evaluate the factors that will affect the horizontal displacement of the shot.   [15 marks]

This is a synoptic extended question because it requires knowledge from two different topics on the specification. Newton's laws of motion are taught under 'Biomechanical principles' and the factors affecting the horizontal displacement of a shot are taught under the 'Projectile motion' section. You need to be aware that there will be synoptic questions in both papers 1 and 2, which can draw from content anywhere in the specification. AO1 4 marks; AO2 5 marks; AO3 6 marks

Student A answer

Newton's first law of inertia states that 'every body continues in its state of rest or motion in a straight line, unless compelled to change that state by external forces exerted upon it' AO1. In terms of the shot it will remain in the thrower's hand in a state of rest until the shot putter exerts a muscular force upon it AO2. Also, the shot will continue to act as a projectile in a state of motion until it hits the ground AO2.

Newton's second law of acceleration states that 'the rate of momentum of a body (or the acceleration for a body of constant mass) is proportional to the force causing it and the change that takes place in the direction in which the force acts' AO1. Force = mass × acceleration (F = ma) AO1 When the shot putter exerts a muscular force to throw the shot the acceleration of the shot or its rate of change of momentum is proportional to the size of the force AO2. So, the more muscular force from the throwing arm the further and faster the shot will go AO2.

As the shot putter throws the shot there are certain factors they need to consider that will affect how far the shot will travel or its horizontal displacement. Firstly, there is the angle of release AO1. The optimum angle of release is dependent upon release height and landing height AO1. When both the release height and the landing height are equal then the optimum angle of release is 45° AO1. If the release height is below the landing height then the optimum angle of release needs to be greater than 45° AO1. When the release height is greater than the landing height, the optimum angle of release needs to be less than 45° AO1. In the shot the release height is greater than the landing height because the shot is released from the hand and the landing height is the ground AO2. Therefore, in order to increase the horizontal displacement of the shot the angle of release needs to be below 45° AO3.

Speed of release is also important AO1. The shot putter needs to exert a large muscular force quickly to increase the horizontal displacement of the shot AO3. Finally, the height of release is the third factor AO1. A shot putter needs to ensure a greater release height because this results in an increase in horizontal displacement, so the shot travels further AO2. The force of gravity is constantly acting on the mass of the shot, so this means the shot should be released at the highest point possible above the ground to gain maximum horizontal displacement AO3. Therefore, the discus thrower needs to follow through, which is achieved by good extension and flexion of the shoulder AO3.

12/15 marks awarded This answer shows thorough knowledge of Newton's laws of motion and the ability to apply those laws to the shot. The factors that affect how far the shot will travel are clearly described, applied and evaluated. Consequently, this answer scores a mark from the top of level 4. With more evaluation this could have been level 5.

Student B answer

Newton's first law of inertia states that 'every body continues in its state of rest or motion in a straight line, unless compelled to change that state by external forces exerted upon it' AO1. So, for example, the shot will remain in the thrower's hand until the shot putter exerts a muscular force upon it AO2. Newton's second law is the law of reaction, where for every action force there is an equal and opposite reaction force. In terms of the shot, the action force comes from the hand.

The factors that affect how far the shot will travel are the height of release AO1, angle of release AO1 and speed of release AO1. With speed of release, a fast throwing arm will mean the shot will go further. AO3

4/15 marks awarded Student B has discussed Newton's third law of motion (law of action/reaction) instead of the second law. Make sure you are aware which law is which, as this is a common mistake. There is not much application or evaluation in the answer, so consequently it only scores a mark from level 2.

■ Sport psychology

Aspects of personality

Question 1

Identify the correct equation used to illustrate the interactionist approach as suggested by Lewin. [1 mark]

A $P = f(D \times H)$

B $B = f(T.E)$

C $P = f(D.E)$

D $B = f(P.E)$

This requires you to know the correct equation. There will be multiple-choice questions in your exam, so you need to follow the instructions on how to answer this very carefully.

Student A answer

D $B = f(P.E)$

1/1 mark awarded This answer is correct. Behaviour is a function of genetic personality traits and experiences gained through social learning.

Student B answer

D $B = f(P.E)$

0/1 mark awarded This answer is correct, but Student B has not followed the instructions and therefore does not gain credit.

Anxiety

Question 2

Evaluate the effectiveness of using observation as a method to measure anxiety. [4 marks]

This question requires you to give advantages and disadvantages of using observation to measure levels of anxiety.

Student A answer

Using observation as a method to measure anxiety is useful because it is a real-life method ✓ that can be used during training and fixtures ✓. However, as soon as you know that you are being observed you will change your behaviour ✓ and it is a highly subjective rather than objective method ✓, which may be time consuming.

4/4 marks awarded This clear answer addresses both advantages and disadvantages of using the observation method.

Student B answer

Observation requires more than one observer ✓, and they need to know how the player is normally ✓.

2/4 marks awarded Two disadvantages are given. However, there are 4 marks available, so two further advantages should be given for full marks.

Aggression

Question 3

Using a practical example, describe how social learning theory can be used to explain aggression in sport. [4 marks]

This requires you to name a specific sporting skill and describe how aggressive behaviour is developed through social learning. Do not waste time on other theories.

Student A answer

Bandura suggested the social learning theory of aggression following his 'Bobo doll' experiment. This experiment showed that aggressive acts are learned through environmental experiences. ✓ Players observe their significant others ✓, such as family, friends, teachers and role models, when they are acting aggressively. If their aggressive act is praised ✓ then the player is likely to copy ✓ the aggressive act the next time they play. The player is more likely to copy someone who is the same age/gender as them. ✓ For example, the player watches his captain punching his opposite prop in a scrum to put him off. When the player is substituted onto the field he imitates the behaviour during the next scrum. ✓

4/4 marks awarded This solid answer demonstrates clear understanding. The example is excellent and illustrates the theory.

Student B answer

Social learning means you watch and copy ✓ other people's aggressive acts. If a person performs a skill aggressively, you will do the same. This is the opposite of trait theory.

1/4 marks awarded This answer is too brief. Stating 'a skill' is not giving a practical example. While social learning is the opposite of trait theory, this is irrelevant to the question.

Motivation

Question 4

Athletes receive a range of rewards in order to motivate them. Describe the types of tangible and intangible rewards that a javelin thrower may receive. [4 marks]

The question requires you to demonstrate that you know the difference between tangible and intangible rewards, and show how a javelin thrower can receive both.

Student A answer

Tangible rewards are physical ✓ rewards that you can touch. The javelin thrower receives a gold medal ✓ for winning. Intangible rewards are invisible — they cannot be seen or felt. They are not physical ✓, for example the praise ✓ the javelin thrower receives from her coach when she throws a personal best distance.

4/4 marks awarded This succinct answer describes tangible and intangible rewards that a javelin thrower might receive.

Student B answer

Tangible rewards are those you can touch. ✓ Intangible rewards are those you cannot. ✓

A footballer may receive a medal or might hear supportive shouts from the stands.

2/4 marks awarded Student B understands the difference between tangible and intangible, and has given brief descriptions that gain credit. However, the examples they have given relate to a footballer rather than a javelin thrower, and therefore will not be credited.

Social facilitation

Question 5

Using practical examples, explain the effects of an audience on a performer, and also suggest strategies to reduce any negative effects that may occur.

[8 marks]

This is an example of an extended question. Remember that for this style of question, the full answer is assessed and a banded marking system is used. Make sure you answer in continuous prose and pay special attention to spelling, punctuation and grammar. Use the correct terminology throughout and support the theory with practical examples. Ensure that you address all parts of the question — describe the effects of social facilitation and social inhibition on a performer, and give strategies to reduce the negative effects.

Student A answer

Social facilitation refers to the effects that a performer experiences when they are being watched. Social facilitation describes the positive effects AO1, i.e. performance gets better. Social inhibition describes the negative effects AO1, i.e. performance worsens.

When people are watching, the performer will experience an increase in arousal AO1. This causes them to revert back to performing their dominant response AO1, which is a well-learned skill. If they are autonomous AO2, for example an elite basketballer AO2, the dominant response will be performed correctly. This is because the performer is experienced and used to performing in front of an audience. If the skill being performed is a simple skill AO2 (e.g. a forward roll) AO2 that does not require a lot of decisions to be made, or if the skill is gross AO2, such as running AO2, i.e. it utilises large muscle groups and does not require a lot of precision, accuracy and control, then the skill will be performed accurately.

Sometimes the presence of spectators has a negative effect on performance. Cognitive AO2 performers, for example a novice gymnast AO2, will not be as successful in front of an audience because they are distracted by it. If the skill is complex AO2, for example passing a ball AO2 (it requires several decisions to be made), and/or the skill is fine AO2, such as a pistol shot AO2 (requiring precision, accuracy and control), then it may be performed incorrectly.

To reduce the negative effects of social inhibition, a range of techniques can be used. Familiarisation AO3 training allows the players to train in front of a crowd so that they get used to it and use strategies to reduce their arousal levels. The player should selectively attend AO3 — focusing on the relevant cues and disregarding the irrelevant distractions to reduce the effects of the crowd. For example, when taking a penalty focus on the ball only and ignore the spectators behind the goal.

The player could utilise cognitive/somatic stress management techniques, such as mental rehearsal AO3 — going over the penalty in their mind AO2 — and progressive muscular relaxation AO3, i.e. working from top to bottom, tensing and releasing each muscle group in turn AO2. Goals should be process and performance-based rather than outcome-based AO3. Finally, encouragement AO2/AO3 should be given to increase self-confidence when performing in front of an audience, for example shouting 'well done' when the performer does correct footwork in netball AO2.

8/8 marks awarded This is an excellent top-band response. Student A has clear and detailed knowledge about the positive and negative effects of social facilitation and inhibition. They clearly have the depth of knowledge required for A-level. The answer is well structured and uses specialist terminology. Clear and accurate links to practical sporting situations are given throughout. A number of strategies to limit the negative effects are given and again are supported with practical examples.

Student B answer

Being watched can make you do better or worse. Experienced performers can do better AO2; new performers will do worse AO2. Zajonc suggested there were passive and interactive others. You can use visualisation AO3 to help. This links to drive theory AO1.

2/8 marks awarded This answer is very brief, lacks depth and structure, and shows limited understanding. The statements made are vague and lack the technical knowledge required to access higher marks. Although four AOs have been identified, the answer is marked holistically and therefore does not achieve higher than level 1.

Group dynamics

Question 6

How can a coach increase the cohesiveness of a team?   [4 marks]

The question requires you to show how a coach creates unity in their team. Your answer should relate to the coach, not the players.

Student A answer

The coach should develop both task and social cohesion by making sure that the players they pick are the ones that work together the best rather than just picking good individuals who play for themselves rather than the team. ✓ The coach should also praise the team when they work together as a unit to achieve the team's goal. ✓ The coach should also make sure that all the squad wears the team's hoodies/training kit when travelling to fixtures because it gives them a collective identity. ✓ During pre-season the coach should organise a team-building day, for example Go Ape, so they get to know each other and become friends. ✓ If everyone knows their specific role and duties ✓ in the team that will also help to bring them together.

4/4 marks awarded This is a great answer, which gives ways to develop both task and social cohesion. Student A also gives more correct answers than marks available, which is good exam technique.

Student B answer

A cohesive team has a clear structure, a common goal and all work together to reach it. Cohesive teams are more successful.

0/4 marks awarded Student B has misread the question and given a definition. Make sure you read everything before you answer anything.

Importance of goal setting

Question 7

Outline the benefits of setting goals.

[3 marks]

This question requires you to state the benefits, but not the principles or types of goal setting.

Student A answer

Setting goals keeps you motivated ✓ and increases confidence ✓. It also controls arousal levels. ✓

3/3 marks awarded This is short, sharp and to the point.

Student B answer

A performer can set process, performance or outcome goals. Process goals aim to improve technique; performance goals aim to improve from last time; outcome goals aim to win.

0/3 marks awarded Student B has misunderstood the question. They have described the types of goal that can be set rather than the benefits of goals.

Attribution and confidence

Question 8

A netball coach asks her wing attack to play out of position and take on the goal attack role for the very first time against a top-level goal defence. The team loses the fixture and the player experiences a loss of confidence. With reference to Weiner's model, analyse the attributions that the player may give. Using Bandura's model, explain how the coach might increase the player's self-efficacy. [15 marks]

> This question requires you to demonstrate your knowledge of both Weiner's and Bandura's models. The question has identified a specific practical example, so this should be referred to throughout your answer. Structure is very important — address each model in a separate paragraph and use the correct terminology.

Student A answer

Attributions are the reasons that the netballer will give when she wins or loses AO1. Weiner suggested that there are four main attributions — ability, task difficulty, effort and luck AO1. The locus of causality says that attributions can be internal or external AO1. Internal attributions, such as ability and effort, are within the netballer's control AO2. For example, the netballer might say that the team lost because she does not have the coordination or perceptual ability to play in the goal attack role AO3. She might also think that the rest of the team did not believe that she could play well as goal attack, and therefore they did not put the effort in, and as she does not like playing there, she did not put as much effort in as normal either AO3.

External attributions such as task difficulty and luck are outside of the netballer's control AO2. The task was made more difficult for her because she was playing against an experienced goal defence when this was the first time she had played as goal attack AO3. She might also suggest that some of the umpire's decisions were incorrect — for example, that she was unluckily to be punished for bad footwork AO3.

The stability dimension describes how permanent the attributions are AO1. Stable reasons such as ability and task difficulty remain the same AO2. This is the perceived low ability of the netballer who thinks that she just is not able to succeed in the goal attack position AO3, and also the difficult task of playing against a tough and experienced goal defence AO3. Unstable attributions such as effort and luck can change from minute to minute and game to game AO2. For example, perhaps at the beginning of the match the player put a lot of effort in trying to move into space quickly AO3. Towards the end of the match perhaps she did not put as much effort in and therefore did not score as many goals. Luck also changes — the netballer could have hit the ring on several occasions rather than scoring AO3.

If the netballer continues to attribute so negatively she might experience learned helplessness **AO1**. This is when she thinks that no matter how hard she tries to play well as the goal attack, she will not succeed **AO2**. Learned helplessness can be global or specific **AO1**. Global learned helplessness relates to all sports, so the netballer would think that she could not succeed in any sport **AO2** — this is not the case in this situation. The netballer is experiencing specific learned helplessness, which means she thinks that she cannot perform well in this position **AO2** because it is not somewhere that she normally plays, and when she did play there, the team lost. As a result, the coach should try to improve her self-efficacy, which is belief in her ability in a specific situation **AO1**, i.e. playing as a goal attack, and her self-confidence, which is more general. In this way her belief in herself to be a good netballer will be improved.

Bandura's model states that self-efficacy is influenced by four factors: performance accomplishments, vicarious experiences, verbal persuasion and emotional arousal **AO1**.

Performance accomplishments mean that the coach can remind the netballer of when she was successful before **AO2**. For example, the coach might recap the results of the shooting drill with the netballer, where she was 100% accurate with her shots **AO3**. This has the greatest effect on the performer according to Bandura, and raises self-efficacy most readily.

Vicarious experiences refer to how the coach highlights other performers completing the same task successfully **AO2**. In this case, the coach might show the netballer videos of her team-mate who made the transition from a wing position to shooter successfully **AO3**. If this player shares characteristics with the netballer, such as gender/age/ability, then this will have a bigger impact on the netballer **AO3**.

Verbal persuasion is about the coach encouraging the netballer. **AO2** The coach should praise the netballer for accurate passing **AO3**, shooting and overall effectiveness as a goal attack. The encouragement from the coach will raise the self-efficacy of the netballer.

Emotional arousal requires the performer to understand and control their arousal/stimulation levels **AO2**. The netballer will have heightened arousal levels because she is playing out of position **AO2**. She should perform stress management techniques, such as mental rehearsal and progressive muscular relaxation **AO3**, to control her arousal levels when playing as a goal attack, and therefore increase self-efficacy.

15/15 marks awarded This is an excellent level 5 response, which demonstrates comprehensive and detailed knowledge of Weiner's model of attribution and Bandura's model of self-efficacy. Practical examples are made consistently to clearly illustrate the points being made. The answer has breadth and depth, is focused and well structured, follows a logical order and addresses all parts of the question set. Correct terminology is used throughout.

Student B answer

When the performer loses, she will think she is not good enough and cannot play netball AO2. This is a type of learned helplessness AO1. She will blame it on her lack of ability and say the task is too difficult AO2. Both of these feature in Weiner's model. Bandura says that you should praise AO2 the netball player when she does well and keep her as calm as possible, which is emotional arousal AO1. If the performer thinks that she put lots of effort in and still lost, she will not be motivated to continue because she thinks she tried her best and was still unsuccessful AO3. Bandura also says that the best way to raise confidence is to tell them what they have done well in the past — their performance accomplishments AO1.

5/15 marks awarded This is a level 2 answer. Student B demonstrates some knowledge but there is limited detail and a lack of breadth and depth. The structure is poor because the answer bounces between Weiner's and Bandura's models. Correct terminology is used infrequently, and the answer lacks coherence.

Leadership

Question 9

Describe when, according to Fiedler, a coach would use a task-orientated style of leadership. [3 marks]

The question requires you to understand Fiedler's model and relate your answer to situations that require a task-orientated style of leadership.

Student A answer

Fiedler stated that a task-orientated style should be used in the most and least favourable ✓ situations. In the most favourable situations, the leader has authority and the respect ✓ of the group. Also, the team members have good relationships ✓ with each other and the task is clear ✓. In the least favourable situations, there is no respect for the leader, and they have no authority. The relationships are poor and the task is not clear.

3/3 marks awarded In describing the most and least favourable situations, Student A clearly understands when a task-orientated style should be used.

Student B answer

When the situation is good or bad. And the leader is respected ✓ and the group know what to do.

1/3 marks awarded This answer is too brief and vague.

Stress management

Question 10

A footballer is asked to take a penalty kick. What negative cognitive and somatic effects might she experience?

[4 marks]

> This question requires you to apply your knowledge. Ensure that you include the cognitive and somatic effects that a footballer experiences when taking a penalty.

Student A answer

The footballer might experience cognitive effects such as negative thoughts ✓ that she might miss the goal, and feel extremely worried ✓. She might also fear the reaction of the crowd. She might notice somatic effects, such as an increase in heart rate and blood pressure ✓ when doing the run up, and might be sweating more ✓.

4/4 marks awarded Full credit is given because the answer explains both cognitive and somatic effects.

Student B answer

- Shakes
- Fear of failure
- Stress

0/4 marks awarded Basic bullet-point answers such as these are too brief, and lack the necessary detail. There is also no link to the footballer/penalty situation, as required by the question.

■Sport and society, and the role of technology in physical activity and sport

Concepts of physical activity and sport

Question 1

Identify the characteristics of sport.

[3 marks]

This question requires you to briefly state a number of features of sport, but with enough detail to illustrate that you clearly understand each point you are making.

Student A answer

The characteristics of sport are:

■ strict rules (e.g. set numbers/set boundaries) ✓

■ officials present to enforce rules ✓

■ rewards received for winning (e.g. extrinsic — trophies) ✓

■ serious/competitive — aim is to win ✓

3/3 marks awarded This shows good exam practice, with four correct points succinctly but correctly made to ensure a maximum mark — try to make more points than marks allocated.

Student B answer

■ Sport has rules.

■ Sport has skills.

■ Sport has lots of benefits, like health and fitness.

0/3 marks awarded The first two points are too vague, for instance 'strict rules' is required, and the third point is irrelevant because it relates to functions, not characteristics.

Question 2

State three characteristics of National Curriculum PE.

[3 marks]

This question requires you to briefly state a specific number of features of PE asked for in the question (i.e. three), avoiding repetition of similar points.

Student A answer

■ It is compulsory. ✓

■ It occurs in lesson time. ✓

■ It is controlled by teachers. ✓

3/3 marks awarded Three correct answers are clearly stated.

Student B answer

■ It occurs in your free time, for example lunchtimes.

■ It is your choice to do it or not.

■ It is delivered by specialist coaches.

0/3 marks awarded The answers stated are all incorrect and relate to school sport.

Development of elite performers in sport

Question 3

Describe the role and purpose of UK Sport in elite performer development. [4 marks]

This question requires you to identify and briefly describe a number of schemes/initiatives UK Sport is implementing to improve success in elite sport.

Student A answer

UK Sport is an organisation that focuses on development of elite performers, and plays a key role in funding them to meet their living and sporting costs via distributing National Lottery funding through the World Class Performance Programme. ✓ It also ensures they are perfectly prepared for the demands of the Olympic Games by providing Olympic preparation camps, such as Belo Horizonte prior to Rio 2016. ✓

Oversight of the Performance Lifestyle programme ensures that elite athletes have expert mentors available to help them meet the competing demands of being an elite performer, as well as continuing with everyday life. ✓ Its funding input into national institutes of sport, such as the EIS, is key to elite performer development because it ensures they have top-class sports facilities and sport science support to maximise their talents. ✓

4/4 marks awarded This describes a number of schemes/initiatives that UK Sport is involved in, which are all important in elite performer development.

Student B answer

UK Sport gives funding to elite performers, such as our top-level cyclists. It also funds anti-doping to ensure that our elite performers are clean athletes. It is important that it works in a coordinated way with other organisations, like NGBs and the EIS, to develop elite performers to the full. ✓

1/4 marks awarded Only three points are attempted for a 4-mark question, which indicates a lack of revision/knowledge of this topic area. The first point is too vague in relation to how UK Sport funds elite performers, whereas the second is not precise enough/linked in a relevant way to the question set. The third and final general point is correct and therefore creditworthy.

Question 4

Explain how the structure of the World Class Performance Programme is supporting the development of elite athletes in the UK. [2 marks]

This question requires you to give a precise description of the main layers of the pathway linked to progression to the podium.

Student A answer

The World Class Performance Programme has two main levels:

1   World Class Podium Potential consists of athletes whose performances have suggested realistic medal-winning capabilities, typically 4–6 years from the podium. ✓

2   World Class Podium is the top end of the pathway, which supports athletes with realistic medal-winning chances at the next Olympic/Paralympic Games (i.e. a maximum of 4 years from the podium). ✓

2/2 marks awarded This gives a clear/correct explanation of the WCPP, as required by the question set.

Student B answer

The WCPP is a funding scheme that operates at podium and podium potential levels.

0/2 marks awarded For an 'explain' question it is important to provide enough detail to illustrate your full understanding of the points made. This answer correctly identifies the two levels of the WCPP, but fails to explain them.

Ethics in sport

Question 5

Define what is meant by the Olympic Oath.   [2 marks]

This requires you to clearly explain the meaning of this sports ethics term.

Student A answer

The Olympic Oath is taken prior to the start of the Games by an athlete/coach/official as representative of all athletes, coaches and officials ✓ at an Olympics. The oath agrees to adhere to key principles of the Olympics, such as fair competition and remaining free from doping. ✓

2/2 marks awarded This answer contains two correct, sufficiently different points in relation to the Olympic Oath.

Student B answer

The Olympic Oath is an out-of-date set of beliefs, which are spoken at the start of an Olympics.

0/2 marks awarded This answer gives an irrelevant opinion on the Olympic Oath, with no detail of who is involved and what is said.

Question 6

Identify which **one** of the following statements best defines gamesmanship. [1 mark]

A Conforming to the unwritten rules, spirit and etiquette of a sport ◯

B Participation in sport for the love of it receiving no financial gain ◯

C Stretching the rules to their absolute limit ◯

D A devotion to sport, involving high levels of physical endeavour with moral integrity ◯

> Sometimes multiple-choice questions are set that require knowledge of the definitions of ethical terms.

Student A answer

C Stretching the rules to their absolute limit. ⬤

1/1 mark awarded Answer 'c' is correct as a definition of gamesmanship.

Student B answer

A Conforming to the unwritten rules, spirit and etiquette of a sport. ⬤

0/1 marks awarded Answer A defines sportsmanship, not gamesmanship.

Violence in sport

Question 7

Using appropriate psychological theories, suggest reasons why sports performers may display acts of violence. Outline and evaluate possible strategies that can be used possible to eliminate such behaviour. [8 marks]

> This is an example of an extended question with a synoptic element, which requires you to link psychological theories of violence from the specification to sports performers, before focusing on how various solutions can be applied to try to eradicate it as much as possible from a sport.

Student A answer

One reason why violence may occur in a game is the frustration-aggression theory . For example, where aggression and violence is due to the need to achieve being blocked . This might be due to poor refereeing in rugby if the opposition are using dirty tackles (e.g. high/late tackles), and the referee does not see this, which may result in a player retaliating and punching an opponent AO2. A strategy to try to overcome violence could be to send the player off and possibly fine the player if that act was highly violent AO1.

However, to be effective, the fine must be 'relevant' to the player's salary, because if a player was fined £1000 and they earned £50000 a week it would not be very effective, and the player might still be violent due to the lack of an effective deterrent AO3.

Another strategy to help decrease such aggressive behaviour due to poor officiating is to use technology to help officials when making decisions AO1. This would help avoid frustration potentially leading to aggressive acts if performers were more confident that correct decisions were being made (e.g. via the TMO in rugby) AO2. Increased use of officiating technology is a highly effective way of decreasing performer aggression because it immediately helps decrease on-field tensions by referring decisions to a neutral official off the field of play AO3.

Another theory of aggression is the aggressive-cue theory, where violence can take place when a socially acceptable cue is present. AO1 For example, in football a coach might encourage over-aggression in their team talk or via shouting from the touchline, encouraging negative deviancy AO2. A strategy that could be used to deter this is to ban the player from future games, meaning they cannot play for a few matches AO2. This could be more effective than fining a player due to the mindset of most athletes giving them a strong desire to compete in all matches AO3.

Instinct theory states that aggressive behaviour is genetic and that the 'violence trait' is within everyone AO1. To try to overcome the natural tendency to violence, a player could work with a sport psychologist and learn how to use strategies such as self-talk/relaxation techniques prior to matches/in training AO2. If specialist sport psychologists are used, and the players work in a positive and receptive way with them, such psychological techniques can be a highly effective way of decreasing violence, particularly with individuals prone to aggressive acts in high-pressure sport AO3.

8/8 marks awarded This is an excellent, highly detailed and well-written answer, with a range of knowledge and application points, and examples clearly illustrating understanding of the points being made. There is also clear/well-argued linkage to evaluative comments that outline the relative effectiveness of various strategies used to try to control player aggression.

Student B answer

Violence is the act of being aggressive, and the intent to harm outside the rules. One reason why a performer might act in a violent way is explained by instinct theory, which suggests that aggression is innate and it comes naturally in a person's genes AO1. Violence can also be linked to the frustration–aggression theory — when a player becomes violent due to a poor refereeing decision, which frustrates them AO1. Aggression can be eliminated by fining players, giving them bans and using positive role models to encourage better behaviour on the field AO1. NGBs can set up education campaigns to educate performers on why they should not act violently AO1.

2/8 marks awarded This answer is too brief and restricted to a limited number of knowledge points, so would score in the bottom band.

Question 8

Using examples, describe the possible causes of football hooliganism. Outline and evaluate various legal measures that football clubs have been required to implement to protect spectators.   [8 marks]

> This is an example of an extended question with a synoptic link, which requires you to outline your knowledge of various causes of violence among football supporters, before focusing on describing the relative effectiveness of various legal measures taken to try and control it.

Student A answer

Football hooliganism was particularly prominent in the 1980s, with intense local rivalries stirred up by media hype being one reason for fan violence AO1. For example, when Norwich played Ipswich there were lots of fights among rival fans due to strong club loyalty to a particular home club in East Anglia AO2.

Violence can also be related to nationalism and religion AO1. At the height of its violence, football hooliganism followed the England team at home and abroad, with lots of fights occurring at international matches/events such as the Euros AO2. Competing religions can also have a strong impact on club loyalties and lead to a hostile atmosphere and crowd violence at matches, for example Celtic vs Rangers (Catholic vs Protestant). AO1/AO2

In the past, poor security/crowd control has led to a lack of segregation, with lots of fights occurring among rival fans AO1.

To try to control football hooliganism, a number of legal measures have been taken and applied by clubs to try to protect fans attending matches.

To improve segregation and keep rival fans apart, top-level grounds have been required (e.g. by the Taylor Report) to make their grounds all-seater AO1. This has a positive impact because fans are allocated seats, with sitting down in separate areas of a ground decreasing their feelings of tension/aggression towards one another AO2. Creating all-seater stadia is therefore an effective way of decreasing hooliganism because it has helped to increase health and safety for fans in grounds, with access to different parts being strictly controlled, keeping rival fans well away from each other AO3.

Increased security via stewarding/legal enforcement (i.e. policing) is another way to control fan violence AO1. CCTV is being used to closely monitor fan behaviour in and around grounds and help ensure their safety AO2. Having more video monitoring and police intelligence, often shared across forces, is a highly effective way to protect fans because any potential trouble can be quickly spotted and effectively dealt with by law enforcement AO3.

7/8 marks awarded This excellent top-band response demonstrates accurate knowledge of a range of relevant causes of football hooliganism, using practical examples to consistently illustrate the points being made. Different legal measures taken to protect fans are then covered, with comments on their relative effectiveness illustrating very high levels of awareness of the points being made. The answer is well focused, and well structured, following a logical order that is linked to the different parts of the question set.

Student B answer

Football hooliganism was at its height in the 1980s, with a number of different causes, including the fact that it provided gangs of mainly males with an outlet to fight AO1.

Sometimes it was linked to politics AO1, for example nationalism and political groups like the National Front promoting themselves at inner-city football clubs, where there was lots of social unrest AO2.

Local derbies, where rivalries were particularly fierce, also caused lots of hooliganism, which was publicised on TV and in the papers AO1.

Protection of fans has been improved in a number of ways, such as fining or deducting points from a club that fails to control its fans. Clubs also work to keep fans apart far more than in the past, again decreasing crowd violence and spectator safety.

2/8 marks awarded This answer is too brief and is mainly restricted to a limited number of knowledge points, so would score in the bottom band. The final two points made are not 'legal measures' taken to control hooliganism, so in terms of this question are irrelevant and cannot be credited.

Drugs in sport

Question 9

Elite performers sometimes break the rules and use banned substances to enhance their performance.

Identify the physiological reasons why they might use (a) beta blockers and (b) EPO to aid their performance.

[4 marks]

This question requires two relevant points to be made that are linked to the physiological (not *psychological*) benefits of each of the banned substances stated in the question.

Student A answer

(a) Beta blockers aid performance physiologically via their ability to counteract adrenaline, which can interfere with performance by binding to nerve receptors ✓, as well as by increasing the blood flow through the arteries ✓.

(b) EPO aids performance by stimulating red blood cell production ✓, increasing the oxygen-carrying capacity of the blood and increasing endurance to help the performer keep working for longer ✓.

4/4 marks awarded Two correct physiological reasons are stated and linked to why elite athletes use beta blockers/EPO to aid their performance.

Student B answer

(a) Beta blockers are good psychologically because they help calm elite performers down in high-pressure situations. They are particularly useful when calmness is required in precision sports like shooting.

(b) EPO is useful for cycling because it helps stimulate red blood cell production. ✓

> **1/4 marks awarded** Part (a) is an irrelevant answer on the *psychological* impact of beta blockers. One relevant point is made on the physiological benefits of EPO.

Question 10

Elite athletes continue to take performance-enhancing drugs despite obvious risks to their health.

Discuss the suggestion that doping is necessary at elite level, and outline and evaluate the strategies that sporting organisations use to limit the use of banned substances by performers.

[15 marks]

> This question requires you to outline different reasons for and against allowing doping into elite sport, before evaluating the potential effectiveness of various strategies that can be used to try and control it.

Student A answer

A number of arguments could be made for allowing doping/drug use in elite sport. These include the fact that it improves physiological capabilities, enhancing performance, and therefore increasing the chances of success via the ability to train longer/more intensely AO1. For example, if an endurance cyclist was allowed to take drugs they could cover more distance in training at higher speeds/intensities and recover more quickly to perform more effectively in their next training session AO2.

You could argue against doping being allowed to improve performance because it is cheating and also has potential serious health risks AO1. This would be the case with power-based athletes (e.g. 100 m sprinters) taking steroids and therefore increasing their risks of blood clots/heart attacks AO2.

Another reason why you could argue that doping should be allowed links to ineffective testing and failure to detect new drugs, which means there is a lack of trust in the system and some athletes might be 'getting away with it', so if drugs were allowed it would level the playing field AO1. However, if you allowed all athletes to take drugs through to elite level it would encourage drugs from an early age, creating negative role models for children and a perception that 'if you don't take it, you won't make it' AO2.

Sports organisations have used various strategies to try to decrease the use of banned substances in sport. Stricter testing systems are being adapted in sports like athletics. **AO1** For example, the 'whereabouts system' requires athletes to inform drug testers from UKAD where they will be for certain periods of time so they can be tested if required to do so **AO2**. To be as effective as possible in limiting the use of drugs, such testing needs to be random and out of competition (i.e. when the athlete least expects it) AO3.

Harsher punishments can be used to act as a deterrent to drugs in sport **AO1**. These include banning someone from a sport, or loss of medals and/or sponsorship/lottery funding. However, in order to be more effective, some people argue that lifetime bans should be used for any athlete testing positive, which is not the case at the moment, with athletes such as Justin Gatlin allowed to return to athletics and win world titles despite previously testing positive for illegal drug use AO3.

Programmes can be developed to educate performers and coaches on the danger of doping and importance of winning in an ethically fair/drug-free manner **AO1**. Sports Coach UK developed Coach Clean as an initiative for coach education on winning fairly and ethically **AO2**. UKAD promotes 100% Me as a campaign to educate coaches/performers, and promote cleaner sport via making positive ethical choices to remain drug free **AO2**. However, when the rewards for winning are so great, athletes and coaches will always be tempted to resort to illegal drugs to increase their chance of winning, so attempts to educate them and develop positive ethics may well fall on deaf ears AO3.

> **12/15 marks awarded** A number of possible reasons for and against allowing doping in elite sport are given, with examples to illustrate the points being made. A range of possible strategies to try to decrease doping in sport are then outlined in depth, with evaluations of their relative effectiveness. The answer is well structured, with a high level of knowledge clearly evident.

Student B answer

At elite level, doping is used to gain a small competitive advantage over opponents. You could argue that drugs such as anabolic steroids should be allowed to increase strength and muscle mass **AO1**. You could also argue that EPO is useful to increase red blood cells and endurance for athletes, such as those in the Tour de France **AO1**.

Most athletes use doping to gain a competitive advantage and develop as physically faster athletes, using drugs as a short-cut to increase their levels of performance **AO1**. Athletes may also dope because their main competitors are taking illegal PEDs, and because they do not want to get left behind while their rivals continue to excel **AO1**.

Strategies used to limit doping by organisations include tougher testing and the fact that if a substance is found in your system you are responsible, even if a coach has pressured you into taking it **AO1**.

Organisations can impose sanctions for players, such as fines and bans, to deter them from doing AO1. For example, in rugby league a player might get banned for a year or two for taking a banned stimulant, but for steroids it might be up to 4 years, as this is something rugby league particularly wants to try to stop AO2.

WADA and UKAD also use out-of-competition testing, which is where they sample athletes as and when they wish AO1.

These organisations might also stop athletes competing in future sporting events if they test positive, i.e. impose a ban from competitive sport AO1. Also, medals, trophies and rewards for winning may need to be returned by those testing positive for banned substances AO1.

4/15 marks awarded Most of the points made could be expanded on, with relevant sporting examples to illustrate more in-depth knowledge/detailed application. No arguments are outlined against allowing doping into sport to provide a balanced answer to the first part of the question. To further improve the answer and gain more marks, there is a need to provide *evaluative comments* on the *relative effectiveness* of various strategies being used to deter doping in elite-level sport.

Sport and the law

Question 11

Explain how a sports coach can ensure that they demonstrate their legal duty of care when working with young performers.

[3 marks]

This question requires three or four points, linked specifically to the steps a coach needs to take to ensure that they meet their duty of care. As an 'explain' question, each point made needs to contain links/examples, to ensure that the points made are backed up by clear explanations.

Student A answer

They can ensure that first aid provision is available, so that any injuries to children can be treated accordingly. ✓ A coach should also make sure that they have received suitable training (e.g. in safeguarding), so that they are fully aware of their legal responsibilities. ✓ It is also important that a coach carries out a risk assessment before they start, to ensure that they have checked for any hazards/dangers (e.g. a wet gym floor). ✓

3/3 marks awarded Three excellent points are made succinctly, including detail/examples to address the requirement to show clear understanding of the points being made.

Student B answer

They should carry out an appropriate risk assessment for the activity being coached to identify any potential dangers (e.g. facility/equipment checks to make sure they are safe for the young performers). ✓

1/3 marks awarded This answer focuses on only one main point, explaining it well, with good use of relevant examples, but ultimately only gaining 1 mark.

Impact of commercialisation on physical activity and sport

Question 12

Outline the positive impact of commercialism on officials. [3 marks]

This question requires you to make a range of different points linked to the benefits of commercialisation for sports officials/referees.

Student A answer

A higher profile increases awareness of the importance of officials for supporting fair play in sport. ✓ Increased wages provide officials with the opportunity to devote themselves full time to officiating (e.g. Premier League football referees). ✓ More funding into a sport like football means that more money is being invested into technology to support officiating, helping them to reach the correct decisions (e.g. VAR). ✓

3/3 marks awarded Three correct points are made, with clear links evident between commercialism and how it has positively impacted on sports officials, for example in football.

Student B answer

Commercialisation of sport is where business principles are applied to sport, linked with sponsorship and the media (i.e. the golden triangle). The golden triangle is important for sport because it brings lots more money into it (e.g. football). This money means that you can afford to employ the best players.

0/3 marks awarded This answer is irrelevant to the question set and therefore earns no marks.

The role of technology in physical activity and sport

Question 13

Define what is meant by GPS technology and, using practical examples, describe the different types of data it provides for sports coaches. [3 marks]

This question requires you to divide your response into two main parts: firstly, to define GPS; and secondly, to describe, using practical examples, the different types of data GPS can provide for sports coaches to use.

Student A answer

GPS stands for global positioning system, and is a type technology that sports performers often wear to track their movements via satellite. ✓ It can provide accurate quantitative data such as speed and distance travelled — for example, in rugby a coach can monitor workload via distance travelled to help gauge fatigue and inform substitutions. ✓ It can also provide qualitative data that are of benefit to coaches, for example when assessing accuracy/quality of passing in football. ✓

3/3 marks awarded GPS is correctly defined before two correct points are made describing the benefits of such technology for sports coaches.

Student B answer

One way in which GPS helps to improve player performance is via their fitness levels. Technology also helps improve clothing for coaches to use with their athletes. Finally, it allows coaches/players to see what they did well, so they can focus on weaknesses.

0/3 marks awarded No definition of GPS is given, so no mark is earned for this. No relevant explanations/examples are used to illustrate how GPS technology can be used to provide coaches with useful performance data.

Question 14

Explain the role of electrostimulation in injury prevention.

[3 marks]

This question requires you to describe, in detail (e.g. using links/examples), how electrostimulation can help prevent injuries occurring.

Student A answer

Electrostimulation helps prevent injuries by strengthening muscles — for example, for a footballer, it can help strengthen the muscle groups in the upper legs to give stability in kicking/tackling actions used in games. ✓ It is also useful because it can help to get rid of lactic acid after a training session by decreasing muscle tension, and reduce the chance of injury by providing a relaxing effect to muscles. ✓

Finally, when recovering from injury and wanting to avoid re-injury, it can help rehab through the gradual strengthening of the muscles that were injured via small incremental increases in workload. ✓

3/3 marks awarded Three correct points are given, with clear explanations of the role of electrostimulation in injury prevention.

Student B answer

Technology is helping injury prevention by:
- helping athletes recover more quickly from training
- helping athletes recover more quickly from injury
- helping athletes improve fitness more quickly

0/3 marks awarded Basic bullet-point answers such as these are too brief and lack the necessary detail to earn marks for an 'explain' question. Moreover, no reference is made to electrostimulation.

Knowledge check answers

1 Someone who leads a sedentary lifestyle will need to eat less food than an active person because they do not need as much energy. An endurance athlete will eat more carbohydrates and unsaturated fats because they need lots of energy for long-duration exercise, and a power athlete will eat more protein because they will put their muscles under more strain due to the explosive nature of their sport.

2 The Cooper 12-minute run involves running, so it is not sport specific for a cyclist. Allthough it will give an indication of VO_2 max, it does not use the muscle groups in the same way. A more valid test would be one using a cycle ergometer.

3 ■ Gradually increase the number of sessions completed per week/or equivalent example.
   ■ Increase the number of work periods in a set/number of sets.
   ■ Decrease the number of rest periods.

4 Fartlek training improves aerobic endurance, which is important for a games player because they predominantly work aerobically during the game. A football game, for example, lasts 90 minutes. However, there are times during a game where intensity is high; this is the same in fartlek training, where intensity is varied. This makes fartlek training more game specific.

5 PRICE: protect the injury; rest to avoid further injury, apply ice for an analgesic effect, which can limit pain and swelling by decreasing blood flow to the injured area; compression and elevation to reduce swelling.

6 ■ More sleep is needed following a heavy exercise programme.
   ■ A deep sleep rebuilds the damage done to muscle cells.
   ■ Blood is directed towards the muscles to restore energy.
   ■ 8+ hours of sleep suggested for an elite athlete.

7 The rugby player can increase the area of their support base by putting one foot in front of the other to widen their stance, flex their knees to lower their centre of mass, and make sure that they position their line of gravity directly between their feet.

8 Second-class lever. This can generate a large force, which is need at take-off because the whole body needs

9 Any two from:
   ■ Air resistance will be acting in opposition to motion, and will depend on the velocity of the sprinter.
   ■ Friction will occur between the runner's spikes and the ground, allowing them to move forward and maximise acceleration.
   ■ Weight (gravity) will occur in a downwards direction from the sprinter's center of mass.

10 Negative impulse occurs whenever the foot is in contact with the ground. This produces a braking action. The longer the contact, the more deceleration occurs.

11 Newton's second law states that the rate of change of angular momentum of a body is proportional to the force (torque) causing it and the change that takes place in the direction in which the force (torque) acts. Therefore, when performing a somersault the diver will continue to spin until they either hit the water or change their body shape. Opening up from a tucked position will slow them down.

12 When moment of inertia increases, angular velocity decreases — and vice versa.

13 Angle of release, height of release and speed of release

14 A drag force acts in opposition to motion and slows something down. The effects of drag can be reduced by reducing cross-sectional area. For example, in cycling this involves crouching low over the handlebars and adopting a streamlined aerodynamic shape, which can be helped by wearing a form-fitting suit and a helmet that extends down to the shoulders.

15 The low, streamlined body position and the shape of the speed skier's helmet creates a flat surface, so the air flow over the top travels a shorter distance, at a slower velocity, than the air underneath. This results in a higher pressure above, therefore creating a downward lift force, which increases friction and melts the snow, thereby increasing velocity.

16 Personality is the 'unique psychological make-up' of an individual. (Gill)

17 $B = f(P.E)$ — behaviour is a function of an individual's personality traits interacting with the environment.

18 Cognitive; affective; behavioural

19 High cognitive anxiety combined with high somatic anxiety.

20 Cognitive anxiety refers to mental symptoms. Somatic anxiety refers to physiological symptoms.

21 When a player feels better and continues to play once aggression is released.

22 Tangible — physical rewards; intangible — non-physical rewards

23 NACH — approach; NAF — avoidance

24 ■ Social facilitation —performance improves when people are watching.
   ■ Social inhibition — performance deteriorates when people are watching.

25 Actual productivity = potential productivity – losses due to faulty processes

26 Process; performance-related; outcome

27 Reasons a performer gives for why they have won or lost.

28 ■ Performance accomplishments
■ Vicarious experiences
■ Verbal persuasion
■ Emotional arousal

29 Natural, innate confidence levels — a generally confident performer

30 ■ Autocratic/task-orientated
■ Democratic/socially orientated
■ Laissez-faire

31 ■ Stress is a negative response, which causes anxiety.
■ Eustress is a positive response to a threat.

32 ■ It is enjoyable and informal in nature; winning is unimportant.
■ It is physically energetic, i.e. involves effort.
■ Participation is voluntary (i.e. choice).
■ It tends to involve adults at the 'participation level' of the sporting development continuum.
■ It is flexible in nature (e.g. numbers participating).
■ It is self-officiated/self-regulated (i.e. decisions during activities are made by the participants themselves).

33 Similarities — both:
■ develop physical skills
■ develop health and fitness
■ help individuals to achieve intrinsic benefits/have fun
Differences:

Physical recreation	Physical education
Voluntary	Compulsory
In free time	In school time
Informal/relaxed	Formal teaching and learning
Self-regulated	Teacher in charge
Limited organisational structure	Highly structured

34 ■ Liaising with other organisations involved in elite performer development, e.g. UK Sport.
■ Organisations with a specific focus on the development of the sport they are responsible for (e.g. elite performer development and winning medals in international sporting competitions).
■ Via promotion of equality of opportunity for all to succeed in their sport.
■ Development of effective talent ID schemes to maintain the talent factory in their sport (e.g. use of regional scouts).
■ Allocation of UK Sport WCP funding/Athlete Performance Awards in relation to their sport.
■ Development of top-level coaches in their sport/developmental coaching structure.
■ Provision of developmental training squads/progressive levels of competition to work through.
■ Provision of support services for elite performers via links with EIS centres (e.g. Performance Lifestyle advice).

35 ■ Offer a range of sport services to NGBs to develop elite performers, including sports science and psychology.
■ Provide Performance Lifestyle advice/personalised support to athletes on the WCPP (e.g. time management and dealing with the media).
■ Provide top-quality/world-class facilities (e.g. high-performance environment to train in, with the best coaches).
■ Used for talent ID assessments — home to the UK Talent Team.
■ Performance innovation (e.g. home to UK Sport's Research and Innovation team, which looks at how technology and engineering can be used to develop kit/equipment to give athletes an edge).

36 ■ Sportsmanship — conforming to the written and unwritten rules, and spirit and etiquette of sport (e.g. kicking the ball out of play when an opponent is injured).
■ Gamesmanship — stretching the rules to their limit (e.g. time wasting when winning).

37 ■ Win ethic and high rewards for success.
■ Importance/emotional intensity of an event (e.g. local derby).
■ Nature of the sport is aggressive (e.g. ice hockey).
■ National governing bodies are too lenient with their punishments.
■ Excitement/over-arousal (e.g. caused by coach team talk); or reaction to crowd abuse.
■ Refereeing decisions are 'poor', leading to frustration.

38 ■ It leads to a decline in participation rates.
■ There is a decrease in live spectator attendances.
■ Supporters are banned from attending matches.
■ All supporters at football matches are treated as hooligans.
■ Teams are banned from competing/docked points/fined, which punishes the football clubs for the acts of their 'fans'.
■ Commercial deals are withdrawn from clubs/players/NGBs due to the poor image of the game.
■ Additional costs to police events can lead to financial pressures on clubs at lower levels of the game.
■ Negative impact on the chances of hosting future major football competitions as a result of damaged reputation.

39 Anabolic steroids:
■ aid in the storage of protein
■ decrease fat in the muscles
■ increase the ability to train for longer/at a higher intensity
■ increase the ability to train more frequently/have a faster recovery time
■ increase muscle size/mass/strength

40 To protect against:
- violent acts of opponents
- contractual issues with employers
- contractual issues with sponsors
- issues linked to equality of opportunity
- unfair NGB decisions/disciplinary actions

41
- Increased performance standards providing a high level of excitement/entertainment.
- Improved quality of facilities resulting from increased investment.
- Improved viewing experience via media innovations (e.g. interactive technology), and the creation of merchandise to create team loyalty via the purchase and subsequent wearing of a team's kit.
- Increased opportunity to watch sport, especially live events, because more competitions, events and matches are taking place.
- Rule changes/variations of a sport's format develop, which provide alternative viewing experiences.
- Increased excitement for the audience while awaiting the decisions of off-field officials (e.g. Hawk-Eye in tennis).

- Increased awareness and knowledge of sport; creation of role models for fans to idolise.
- Increased elimination of the negative aspects of sport (e.g. player violence).

42
- Indirect calorimetry is the measurement of the amount of heat and energy generated in an oxidation reaction.
- A metabolic cart is a device for measuring the body's metabolism by calculating the amount of heat produced.

43
- Increased sense of crowd excitement/involvement, for example awaiting decisions via a big screen (e.g. Hawk-Eye).
- Improved experience of watching sport at home (e.g. HD/split-screen coverage).
- Increased excitement from watching top-level performances resulting from technological advancements.
- A wider range of sports becomes more accessible as a result of media advancements/satellite technology.